Courage to Be Me — Living with Alcoholism

By Alateen Members and Sponsors

For information and catalog of literature
write World Service Office for Al-Anon and Alateen:

Al-Anon Family Group Headquarters, Inc.
1600 Corporate Landing Parkway
Virginia Beach, Virginia 23454-5617
757-563-1600   fax 757-563-1655

Library of Congress Catalog Card No. 96-C79465
ISBN 0-910034-30-3

Publisher's Cataloging in Publication

Courage to be me--living with alcoholism / Al-Anon Family
Groups.
p.cm.
Includes index
ISBN 0-910034-30-3

1. Alcoholics--Family relationships. 2. Children of Alcoholics. 3. Al-Anon Family Group Headquarters, Inc. I. Al-Anon
Family Group Headquarters, Inc.

Approved by
World Service Conference
Al-Anon Family Groups

1-50M-96-9.00   B-23   Printed in U.S.A.

THIS BOOK BELONGS TO :

Stephanie Dickson

I GOT IT ON:

Day___?___Month_March_Year_97_

This book is written by and for all the thousands of young
people who have been or are still affected by another
person's drinking. May they find peace, serenity
and recovery in the pages that follow.

SUGGESTED ALATEEN PREAMBLE TO THE TWELVE STEPS

Alateen, part of the Al-Anon Family Groups, is a fellowship of young people whose lives have been affected by alcoholism in a family member or close friend. We help each other by sharing our experience, strength and hope. We believe alcoholism is a family disease because it affects all the members emotionally and sometimes physically. Although we cannot change or control our parents, we can detach from their problems while continuing to love them. We do not discuss religion or become involved with any outside organizations. Our sole topic is the solution of our problems. We are always careful to protect each other's anonymity as well as that of the alcoholic.

By applying the Twelve Steps to ourselves, we begin to grow mentally, emotionally and spiritually. We will always be grateful to Alateen for giving us a wonderful, healthy program to live by and enjoy.

TABLE OF CONTENTS

TABLE OF WORKSHOPS

BEFORE WE BEGIN . . .

Many of us in alcoholic families learned to toughen up and to grow up very quickly. Or else we found ways to disappear, and we found places deep inside ourselves to hide our feelings. We felt as if we had to do these things just to protect ourselves, because we felt alone.

And then we found Alateen.

In Alateen we discover that there is a safe place where we can come every week to let our guard down. We can relax and be ourselves. We can tell the truth. We can cry. We can laugh. Or we can just listen.

When we stick with the program for a while, our attitudes start to change; problems become easier to deal with and our lives start to become manageable.

Little by little, we get courage from our Alateen friends, and we get courage from our Alateen sponsors. We get the courage to be ourselves, to be kids, to be teenagers and to be young adults. We no longer feel alone.

This book is a collection of sharings and artwork from Alateen members all over the world. Like Alateens everywhere, we share our experience, strength and hope with other Alateen members.

And we get to take what we like — and leave the rest.

WHAT IS ALCOHOLISM?

The American Medical Association recognizes alcoholism as a disease that can be arrested but not cured. One of the symptoms is an uncontrollable desire to drink. Alcoholism is a progressive disease. As long as alcoholics continue to drink, their drive to drink will get worse. If the disease is not arrested, it can end in insanity or death. The only method of arresting alcoholism is total abstinence.

Alcoholism is a lifetime disease. Most authorities agree that even after years of sobriety, alcoholics can never again control their drinking once they start.

There are many successful treatments for alcoholism today. Alcoholics Anonymous is the best known and widely regarded as the most effective. Alcoholism is no longer a hopeless condition, provided it is recognized and treated.

(from *Alateen: Hope for Children of Alcoholics*, page 3)

The Effects of Alcoholism
ON THE FAMILY AND FRIENDS

While most of us know that alcoholism is a disease, we may not recognize it as a disease that affects the entire family physically, emotionally and spiritually.

Sometimes we feel responsible for the problem drinking itself. We are hurt and upset and respond with resentment, bitterness and fear. Our determined, angry or fearful efforts to do something about it don't help. Sometimes our own behavior is inappropriate. We scream, cry, yell, plead, pray, threaten or refuse to communicate. We make excuses and protect the alcoholic.

While we are so focused on the drinking and the behavior of the alcoholic, we don't realize that other members of our family are affected too. It is easy to see the direct impact of the alcohol on the drinker. We don't understand how the non-drinking parent can have a problem when they aren't the one who is drinking. They are "just weird." The effects of alcoholism on each family member and their relationships to the alcoholic and each other are very individual. We may get to Alateen because one parent drinks, but we eventually come to realize how the disease of alcoholism has affected our entire family.

It seems that no matter what we try, we are unable to make lasting improvements. Still, we continue to try to stop the alcoholic's drinking. Many of us want to escape even to the point of taking our own lives.

The best ways to deal with alcoholism are to gain knowledge and change our attitudes. The Alateen/Al-Anon program is a spiritual way of life based on the Twelve Steps of Alcoholics Anonymous. Study of the Alateen program and its Twelve Steps strengthens us, guides us and gives us the knowledge and tools to change our lives for the better.

SERENITY PRAYER

God, grant me the Serenity to accept
the things I cannot change,
Courage to change the things I can,
and Wisdom to know
the difference.

COURAGE

It takes courage to try something new. When we have the courage to try Alateen, we find that our courage to handle difficult situations can improve as well.

Alateens share on
COURAGE

I used to think that I didn't have any courage.

Every time I saw my alcoholic stepfather, I kind of backed away. I'd go into the den or into the bathroom, and I'd lock the door behind me. So I really thought I didn't have any courage.

But now I know I do have courage. I have the courage to take care of myself. And in Alateen, I've learned that I'm not alone.

✍

I've been in Alateen for almost a year. I can't even begin to say how much Alateen has changed my life.

I remember my first meeting. I cried most of the time, but somehow I found the courage to talk.

I told a bunch of total strangers my biggest secret. And the weird thing about it was that nobody laughed at me, the way I was used to people laughing at me at home. They just sat there and listened. And they understood too.

I never really had anyone treat me like that before. My mom was never there to listen to me. She was either too drunk or too high.

From my very first meeting in Alateen, I knew I'd found some people I could trust. They're wonderful to me. I look forward to seeing them every week. I know they won't laugh at me, no matter what I say — even if I cry through the whole meeting.

I can say everything I want to say, without holding anything back.

I come to Alateen for me, not for my mother or father or anyone else — for me. Alateen helps me cope with all of the alcoholics in my life, one day at a time.

✍

I used to be a lonely and scared little girl, wishing I was dead. I felt like life just wasn't worth living anymore. I hurt too much. So many people told me that they were always there for me — but I wanted to keep my problems all to myself. I didn't want to bother anyone.

Well, that was very true about me. That's the kind of person I was. Maybe I still am like that, once in a while, deep down inside.

Why not? Alcoholism tore my family apart. The alcoholic was never there, and the non-alcoholic was always there without ever really being there, if you know what I mean.

It took a lot of courage for me to reach out for the help I needed. I felt so scared all the time. I felt scared at home and at school, and sometimes I even felt scared when I was with my friends. I remember I felt really scared sometimes when I was all alone.

I ended up in the hospital because of my suicidal feelings and my depression. Well, after I got out of the hospital I worked bit by bit to get my life back together.

I got a lot of help from a lot of friends. I got a lot of new friends. I got a lot of chances to hear how other people dealt with their own feelings of being lost and feeling worthless and afraid. Alateen accepted me, and I got additional help from my pastor, counselors, family, and other friends too. I didn't have to keep anything a secret in Alateen. Nobody minded where I was getting help, as long as I was getting it. I can't tell you how happy the Alateen welcome made me. I've changed a lot by working the Twelve Steps of Alateen, but nobody made me do it. It's not like homework or tests at school. The only test that counts is how I feel. Believe me, I feel glad to be alive. Thanks everyone. Thank you very much.

When I asked my dad to help me with something, he blew up in my face. I wasn't sure what to say, but I knew if I said anything it would get me into trouble. So I went to my room to sulk. A few minutes later, he knocked on my door. He apologized for blowing up at me. I thanked him for admitting he was wrong and for coming to tell me.

My dad thought I was being sarcastic, but I told him I wasn't—I never would have been able to admit that without Alateen! Speaking out at the meetings has given me courage to talk freely. Even though I'm still scared of my dad, I find it's getting easier to talk with him about my feelings. I have yet to talk with my dad about his drinking, but hopefully I'll be able to do that pretty soon.

Alateen has really gotten me far. I'm not just coming for my father now. I'm coming for me.

Workshop on
COURAGE

Complete the following sentences, adding as many sentences as you want.

To me courage is ...

I realized I had courage when I ...

Before Alateen I had courage to ...

Since coming to Alateen I have courage to ...

Courage is important because ...

What I have the most courage to do or say is...

The hardest things for me to do or say are ...

I show courage by ...

KINDS OF ALATEEN MEETINGS

In Alateen, each group is autonomous. That means that we are in charge of our own meetings. When our group makes a decision it means that all of the members get a voice and a vote. One of the things that a group can decide is what kind of meetings to have.

There are a lot of different kinds of meetings in Alateen, including:

Newcomer's Meetings
Twelve Steps Meetings
Slogans Meetings
Twelve Traditions Meetings
Topic/Discussion Meetings
Twelve Concepts Meetings
Al-Anon and AA Guest Speaker Meetings
Personal Stories Meetings
Panel Discussion Meetings
Literature Meetings
Exchange Meetings
Outside Speaker Meetings
Open Meetings
Group Inventory Meetings
Closed Meetings

Helpful descriptions for each of these kinds of meetings can be found in *A Guide to Alateen Sponsorship - An Unforgettable Adventure* (P-86) or in Al-Anon guideline G-13, Suggested Programs for Meetings. Guidelines are available at most local Al-Anon literature distribution centers and through the Al-Anon World Service Office.

While a group may usually hold a particular type of meeting, there are advantages for a group to vary its weekly format. By combining different kinds of meetings, the members can get a little bit of what they really like at each meeting. And many groups have different Alateen members at their meeting every week.

The following suggested meeting format includes the basic elements used regularly by many groups. Following the suggested meeting format is a list of alternate additions. As each meeting progresses, the members can decide to add one or more of these items, spend more time on one section, or choose a different alternate item each week. They can decide to try something completely new, or not even read the suggested format.

Why do we have so many choices? Because for many groups that are new or for groups that have a lot of newcomers each week, it's a lot easier to change the meeting a little bit, than it is to start all over each week. Just about everyone wants to help the newcomers get a good start in Alateen, but hardly anyone wants to have the same Newcomers' Meeting every single week.

Feel free to adjust this format in any way that is agreeable to the members of your group.

SUGGESTED ALATEEN MEETING FORMAT

1. Hi! My name is ___(First name only)___, and I'm your chairperson for tonight. Would all who care to, please join me in a moment of silence, followed by the Serenity Prayer (on page 12).

2. The chairperson reads the ALATEEN SUGGESTED WELCOME*:

   > We welcome you to the _____ Alateen Group and hope you will find in this fellowship the help and friendship we have been privileged to enjoy.
   >
   > We who live or have lived with the problem of alcoholism understand as perhaps few others can. We, too, were lonely and frustrated, but in Alateen we discover that no situation is really hopeless, and that it is possible for us to find contentment and even happiness, whether the alcoholic is still drinking or not.
   >
   > We urge you to try our program. It has helped many of us find solutions that lead to serenity. So much depends on our own attitudes, and as we learn to place our problem in its true perspective, we find that it loses its power to dominate our thoughts and our lives.

Adapted from the Al-Anon suggested welcome

The family situation is bound to improve as we apply the Al-Anon/Alateen ideas. Without such spiritual help, living with an alcoholic is too much for most of us. Our thinking becomes distorted by trying to force solutions, and we become irritable and unreasonable without knowing it.

The Al-Anon/Alateen program is based on the Twelve Steps (adapted from Alcoholics Anonymous) which we try, little by little, one day at a time, to apply to our lives along with our slogans and the Serenity Prayer. The loving interchange of help among members and daily reading of Alateen and Al-Anon literature thus make us ready to receive the priceless gift of serenity.

Al-Anon/Alateen is an anonymous fellowship. Everything that is said here, in the group meeting and member to member, must be held in confidence. Only in this way can we feel free to say what is in our minds and hearts, for this is how we help one another in Alateen.

3. Do we have anyone here for their very first Alateen meeting? If so, would you introduce yourself by your first name only so that we can welcome you?

4. Now, can we go around the room and have everyone introduce themselves by their first name only?

5. Who would like to read Alateen's Twelve Steps? (or pass them around, each member reading one Step).

6. Who would like to read Alateen's Twelve Traditions? (or pass around, each member reading one Tradition)

7. Are there any Alateen announcements?

8. Tradition Seven: We will now pass the basket. There are no dues or fees in Alateen, but we are a self-supporting group and we need money for expenses like rent, literature and to support our district, area and World Service Office.

9. Chairperson chooses a kind of meeting, based on a reading or discussion topic (alternate format additions are listed below)

10. When there are only a few minutes left in the meeting the leader reads the ALATEEN SUGGESTED CLOSING:

> In closing, I would like to say that the opinions expressed here were strictly those of the person who gave them. Take what you liked, and leave the rest.
>
> The things you heard were spoken in confidence and should be treated as confidential. Keep them within the walls of this room and the confines of your mind.
>
> A few special words to those of you who haven't been with us long. Whatever your problems, there are those among us who have had them too. If you try to keep an open mind you will find help. You will come to realize that there is no situation too difficult to be bettered and no unhappiness too great to be lessened.
>
> We aren't perfect. The welcome we give you may not show the warmth we have in our hearts for you. After a while, you'll discover that though you may not like all of us, you'll love us in a very special way — the same way we already love you.
>
> Talk to each other, reason things out with someone else, but let there be no gossip or criti-

cism of one another. Instead, let the understanding, love and peace of the program grow in you one day at a time. Will all who care to join me in closing with the _____ prayer?

It is suggested that groups close in a manner that is agreeable to the group conscience.

11. Most groups end by holding hands in a circle and closing with a prayer, followed by hugs and fellowship.

Remember, the purpose of the suggested meeting format is to help you and your group to get things started. Feel free to change it to suit your group's needs. One suggestion is to use one of the alternate additions below each week.

ALTERNATE ADDITIONS TO THE SUGGESTED FORMAT:

- The role of sponsors in an Alateen meeting: Our Alateen sponsors are responsible members of Al-Anon who share their experience, strength and hope. They provide direction in the Alateen meeting to help keep the focus on the Al-Anon program of recovery. To the best of their ability they maintain an atmosphere of safety from emotional or physical harm. Alateen sponsors offer guidance without dominance and encourage us to take responsibility for our own actions.

- Would anyone like to read "What Is Alcoholism?" (on page 10)

- Would anyone like to read "Reflections"? (on page 314)

- Who would like to share with the newcomers what it was like when you came to Alateen, and why you keep coming back?

- Let's go around the room sharing one good thing and one bad thing that happened this week.

- Who would like to read the "Introduction to the Twelve Steps of Alateen"? (on page 82)

- Would anyone like to share their experience with one of the Twelve Steps? (Or read a sharing on one of the Steps from pages 82-182.)

- Would anyone like to share their experience with one of the Twelve Traditions? (Or read a sharing from pages 183-268.)

- Would anyone like to share how they solved a problem this week?

- Would anyone like to suggest something new or different to do at today's meeting?

- Would anyone like to read today's page in *Alateen: A Day at a Time?*

- For other topic ideas, consult the index of *Alateen—A Day at a Time*, *Alateen—Hope for Children of Alcoholics*, or other Alateen literature. *A Guide to Alateen Sponsorship: An Unforgettable Adventure* also contains meeting planning and topic suggestions.

Workshop On
MEETING FORMAT

Complete the following sentences, adding as many sentences as you want.

What I like best about my Alateen meeting is ...

Some other things I like about my Alateen meeting are ...

Since I am responsible for helping improve my Alateen meeting, I could ...

As a newcomer, the meeting helped me by...

Note: Some groups have used this type of format for a successful group inventory!

NEWCOMERS: WE KNOW HOW YOU FEEL

Coming to a meeting for the first time is a scary experience. Many of us come to our first meeting because we have to, not because we want to. We are scared, shy and would rather be anywhere else on earth. These unknown people can't possibly understand our problem.

By sharing how we felt during our first days and weeks in the program we begin to build a bridge for the newcomers. We invite them to join us because we too were standing there once ourselves. We do know how they feel.

Alateens share on
NEWCOMERS

I used to feel very, very angry about my mother's drinking. I also thought that I was the only one who had a family that had alcoholic problems.

When I first came to Alateen I couldn't believe how many kids had the same problems in their families that I had in mine.

I'm just glad I'm not alone.

I used to feel left out, like I had no friends. Even my family members weren't able to be friends with me, yet.

My mother had been going to AA for a little while. I think I saw some changes in her, but she was gone a lot of the time. She loved her meetings, and she went to a lot of them, but if she missed a week or two of meetings, then she'd yell and act crazy.

Then one day, when I couldn't stay home alone, my mom took me to her meeting. While I was there I met a man who was sponsoring an Alateen group. I had no idea at the time how much this was going to mean to me.

I had no idea that I was going to start to feel what it was like to be loved. I didn't know that I was going to learn how to give love to others. I didn't know that I was going to cry my eyes out when I found out that people already loved me. They did. They loved me for no reason, just because I was me. I didn't have to do anything for it.

In my whole life, I never thought love was important. I didn't know that love could make a person happy. Before Alateen I always said I'd never love anyone because I didn't want to get hurt. I thought if I loved someone, then I'd lose them.

In Alateen I've learned how good it feels to love and to be loved. I feel happy.

When I first found out about how bad drinking was, I felt scared. Then I began to notice things about my parents that I'd never noticed before.

So I began to think, "Should I just wait, or should I ask them about it?"

Finally, I made up my mind. I decided to talk with them

about their drinking. And I did talk with them. But all I ever heard was, "I can't help it." So then I started to forget about it. But a few years later I couldn't help worrying. So I began to talk with them about it again. Then my dad started going to AA meetings. It really made me feel good for him to go.

After about a year, my dad said he thought I should try going to an Alateen meeting. So I did, and now I'm even happier than I was before.

I came to Alateen through a school guidance counselor. I was having major problems at home. My mom and her boyfriend were constantly fighting. Then my mom ended up leaving home to go to a mental hospital because she was going to kill herself. The next day I went to school and pretended everything was all right.

My best friend knew something was wrong, but I didn't want to tell her about it. Then I received a notice to go to the guidance counselor's office. The guidance counselor told me my mom's boyfriend called to see if I was all right. He wanted to see if I would talk to the counselor about what had happened the night before.

After I told the counselor almost my whole life story, she told me about Alateen. I'm sure glad somebody had told her about Alateen so she could tell me. Now my life is getting back to where I can handle it, one day at a time in Alateen.

✍

Newcomers have taught me how to live and let live. I get to share with them what has worked for me and then let them make their own choices. We talk to each other and reason things out, but we get to do our own footwork. Seeing the lights come on in someone else's eyes and watching the walls come down remind me of where I came from and proves over and over that this program works.

✍

My friend knew that my father had a drinking problem. One day before my third period class in school my friend came up to me and asked me if I wanted to attend a meeting with her. She told me her father had the same problem and that an Alateen meeting could help me.

Before I went to Alateen I couldn't even get next to my father without him hitting me or putting me down. He said he didn't know why my mother ever had me, because all I did was bring problems to my family. Each time this happened I'd always end up crying.

So I went to Alateen with my friend. The meeting helped me a little bit that first day. I learned not to argue with him when he is drinking. And it helped a little bit more every time I went. Sometimes I can talk with my father about his problem. He hasn't hit me in over three years, and I hope he never will again.

Thanks Alateen.

✍️

I guess the first time I realized there was a problem was when my parents were having a party with their old high school friends. Even their friends didn't pay any attention to their own children, because they were so drunk.

I was left to take care of about eight children, all under four years old, and I was only eight. I can remember at one time during the party that my mother had disappeared and my dad was passed out. Later, I heard my dad come downstairs and start to throw up. I felt really scared.

This is what it was like before my parents went to AA and before I came to Alateen. I think it was a good idea for all of us to go to meetings, so everyone in my family could get better at the same time.

When my parents said they were going to quit drinking, I didn't know quite what to think. I'd heard this same thing before, only to find out later that they didn't really mean it. In the end, I just got hurt.

But this time was different. For one thing, this time they brought me to Alateen.

I didn't know that I could get help. I just thought I'd always have to do everything all by myself. But so many people have helped. It's still kind of hard to believe that people I never knew before would really care about me and my family.

I have feelings now that I never thought I would ever have. I love lots of people, and they love me. When they ask me how I'm feeling, they really want to know how I'm feeling. And when I tell them how I'm feeling, they really listen.

I never thought I'd ever end up having a wonderful life, but I have a wonderful life right now.

I heard about Alateen from a good friend. When she told me about it, I wasn't so sure that I wanted to go. I just decided to give it a try.

When I got to my first meeting I felt out of place. I didn't think anybody would have the problems I had, but I found out they did. Everyone cared, shared, and listened. I met lots of people at my first meeting. I really enjoyed it, so I kept coming back.

When my mom was drinking I felt it was my responsibility to do all of the stuff that she was supposed to do. I found out in Alateen to just take care of me.

I have more friends now than I've ever had, thanks to Alateen.

I came to Alateen because I thought it might help. And it does. It's fun, and I'm going to keep coming back.

Alateen is a work of art!

When my mother started drinking again, I tried to get out of the house as quickly as possible. I used my neighbor's phone to call one of my Alateen friends to see if I could find a safe place to spend the night. Two times my mother had gotten violent with me after she got drunk, and I wanted to do whatever I could to keep her from hurting me anymore.

All my life I've been surrounded by relatives who are alcoholics. A couple of years ago, my parents separated because of my mother's drinking. During that time my mother stopped drinking, and she was getting her life back in shape.

I was proud of her. I was hoping she would start a new life. But my parents got back together again. Things returned to normal, unfortunately. Fortunately for me, however, I've been going to Alateen. I don't feel alone anymore. No matter what happens with my family or with my mother, I've got people I can count on now. I'm glad I came here.

When I came to Alateen for the first time, my life was a total mess. I felt like I was completely worthless. I hoped Alateen could help me deal with my problems without overreacting. I'm trying to learn how to keep an open mind and not take everything so personally. The more meetings I go to, the better I feel.

I didn't know who I was before I came to Alateen. I acted like someone else so I could get people to be friends with me. As a result, I never really got to know what I was like.

Now that I'm in Alateen, I've realized that it's okay to be who I am. If people don't like who I am, that's their problem.

I also realized that it's good to cry sometimes. And it's real good to take time for myself.

Thanks to Alateen, I know who I am, and I love that person very much. I guess you could say that's why I'm in Alateen.

Before Alateen, I was afraid and very unsure of myself. I felt confused about my feelings and about my position in my family.

As I started coming to Alateen, I became more aware of my feelings. I was able to start expressing them, whether they were good or bad, without being afraid to tell the whole story.

Living with an alcoholic hasn't been very easy for me. I'm just trying to apply the Twelve Steps to my home life. My hope is that one day I will know where I stand with my fa-

I WAS trash until I came to ALATEEN!

ther. Maybe I'll be able to talk about my feelings toward him and his drinking.

Alateen has been the best thing to come into my life. I'm reaching for a new beginning, and I feel like I'm on the right track.

🖐

I couldn't talk to anyone before I came to Alateen. And I blamed myself for everything. I've only been coming to Alateen for about six months, but I've learned that it's not right to blame myself for everything. And I've learned that as soon as I can talk about what's going on with me, then I'll feel better.

🖐

I'm 14 years old, and I live in a small town. I was very young when my mom started drinking.

Mom just couldn't control herself after her first drink. She'd beat me and leave me at home all by myself. Then she'd come home real late at night.

It got so bad I couldn't stand to be in the same room with my mom. I secretly smelled her breath when I kissed her to see if I was going to be safe.

I was so sick of her drinking that I started running away from home. I thought about committing suicide, and I thought about killing her. Finally, I ended up in a mental hospital.

My mom swore she would quit drinking, so I came back home. But she started drinking again.

Then my mom went to AA, and I started coming to Alateen. Thanks, everyone, for helping me.

I used to do very well in school. In fact, I was one of the brightest kids in my class. I was well-behaved, popular. I always hung out with a good crowd. I never got into any kind of trouble. Actually, I was too afraid to get into any trouble.

When school was out I used to wait at the corner. This was the hardest part of my day. I was waiting for my mom to pick me up, but I didn't know what to expect.

As soon as she arrived I could tell if she had been drinking. Her voice sounded muffled. Her face looked pale. From the first minute I was with her I could tell what the rest of the night was going to be like. I knew when my dad came home he was going to fight with her. He'd argue, yell, scream, and then he'd run away.

But one afternoon my mom didn't show up at all. I waited as long as I could. I kept picturing her in different ways. When she hadn't been drinking she'd be smiling, wearing make-up; she'd even look pretty. When she was drunk she'd be cold, tired, quiet, too quiet.

I couldn't believe that she wouldn't show up at all. Finally I decided to walk home. It was a long way to walk, and I hadn't done it before, but I figured I must be old enough because by then I'd been taking care of my little sister for quite awhile.

I'd been doing a lot of things for quite awhile, like covering up for my mom at home. You know, I did things around the house that she should have been doing. I never told anybody about all the bottles of alcohol I found at our house. I never told anybody anything about my family, but I did everything I was told to do. I obeyed all of my teachers and coaches and scout leaders. It was like I felt like I needed to be perfect just to keep bad stuff from happening at home.

I never told anyone about the night my mom didn't come to pick me up from school. Since then I've thought if I could have gotten into Alateen when I was real young, maybe I wouldn't have had to keep things bottled up inside of me for so long.

I didn't tell anybody about my mom for a long, long time. I wish I would have told somebody, but I didn't know anybody cared, until I finally found Alateen. Everything I needed was right there waiting for me.

Thanks, everybody, for letting me talk.

✍️

When I first came to the program I thought it was stupid. I thought my family was normal and I didn't need to come here.

Then I thought they were telling me that my dad was to blame for all the problems I had. So that's what I did. I blamed everything on my dad.

After about my fifth meeting, I realized that my problems were my problems. It wasn't my dad's fault. In fact, the big problem in his life and my life was alcoholism.

✍️

Now when my dad yells or screams at me, I just say to myself, "Girl, he's sick. Don't yell back. Just leave him alone until he's sober."

When I was really little my dad used to drink every minute of every day. At least once a week my mom would throw my dad's clothes out the window, and my dad would sleep outside.

I didn't understand what alcoholism meant then. I always thought it was my fault that my dad drank, because he used to blame it on me. As I got a little older I started to think that I knew more about alcoholism. It didn't help though, because I still had the same kind of empty feeling inside.

Later on, my dad didn't drink as much as before. When he wasn't drinking he'd try to be nice, but I couldn't even look at him without all of my horrible memories coming back. It got to where I just wanted to hide in my room. Then one day I heard about an Alateen group that started at my school. I decided to go because I thought it might help.

Every time I go to Alateen I feel a little bit better about my dad's drinking problem. I've stopped yelling at him as much as I used to. I've always hated his drinking, but now I understand it. I understand that my dad loves us and that he doesn't want to hurt us, but he can't help it.

I'm glad I came to Alateen. I've even come closer to God because of my group. I'm doing the best I can to live according to the Steps and the Traditions and the Slogans. And I've learned that I'm not the only kid who has an alcoholic family member. It makes me feel good to know that I'm not alone.

My father drank beer. I thought that was normal. I thought all dads drank beer when they were driving a car. I thought all refrigerators had two or three cases of beer inside. And didn't all dads yell at moms? Didn't all moms yell at their kids? Needless to say, I was really messed up when I walked into my first Alateen meeting.

What I wasn't at all prepared for, or used to, was the love that I found in the program. Before I came to Alateen I'd been having a real hard time with guy-girl relationships. I discovered that I was looking for my mother in the girls that I thought were attractive. I guess I tried to find in girls the love that I didn't get from my mom. I think I figured if mom didn't love me then maybe a girl would.

I had to stop looking to others to love me. I had to start loving myself. My home group really helped. The Twelve Steps and Twelve Traditions did too. And a little exercise that I got from my sponsor also helped. My sponsor suggested that every morning when I wake up I might look in the mirror and tell myself that I love me. At first I didn't believe it. I laughed and felt stupid. But I kept doing it, and I tried to believe.

Guess what? It worked! I love myself! And I remember... "It works when I work it, so I work it — because I'm worth it!"

I'm writing from the state hospital. My father is an alcoholic. When I was little, my father sexually and physically abused my sister and me.

When I got taken away from my family for my own protection, I started hurting myself in many different ways, including drinking and abusing myself physically. I know it's hard for people to understand why I would do that, but I did it.

I still have a very hard time controlling myself. I was hurt so much when I was little that it feels like that's what's supposed to happen to me now. If someone else won't do it to me, then I'll do it to myself.

The thing that's different for me is that I've been to some Alateen meetings. The other thing that's different is that I have a lot of time to think about things here in the hospital. I know I can get better. I know I can get some help, but do you know what I really want? I want somebody from Alateen to come and see me while I'm here. I wish somebody would start an Alateen meeting in every state hospital in the whole world.

Workshop On
NEWCOMERS

Complete the following sentences, adding as many sentences as you want.

When I first came to Alateen my attitude was ...

Now that I have been in Alateen, I feel differently about ...

The first thing I learned in Alateen was ...

As a newcomer, the program helped me to ...

BEFORE AND AFTER ALATEEN

The program has changed our lives. We can remember what it was like before Alateen. Often those memories are painful. But Alateen has changed us and our outlook; our understanding and our approach have changed. We have a better life now than we did before.

Alateens share on
BEFORE AND AFTER ALATEEN

I'm a beginner in Alateen, and I haven't really begun to work a program yet. But that doesn't mean I haven't learned anything.

My father destroyed my confidence and spirit. He's a real loud alcoholic who acts like a bully, especially toward people who are smaller than he is. In the short time I've been coming to Alateen I've found a way to accept the way my father is. When he does the same old things that he's always done, I pretend that he's got the worst toothache in the world. I wouldn't hate him for having a terrible toothache, so why should I hate him for having a terrible disease like alcoholism?

Now I can respect my father, because he is my father. And I can start taking care of myself, thanks to Alateen. I can hope that my dad gets better so maybe he'll feel better too. But I don't have to wait for him. I can see how I'm going to start feeling better from now on.

Before I came to Alateen my moods changed all the time. I felt scared. I laughed when I felt like crying. Everything was mixed up. I did things to make people see that I needed help—without coming out and asking anybody to help me.

Now that I've been in Alateen for over a year, I feel different. I can understand better why people act the way they do. And I don't judge them so much. My Alateen program helps me avoid resentments and holding grudges. I guess I've quit blaming myself and others for the things that are totally out of our control.

In Alateen I've found friends to share stories with about yesterday. I've also found friends that I can share hopes with about tomorrow. I've found reasons to live and reasons to reach out and help other people, even the alcoholic.

Before I came to Alateen I hurt a lot. I didn't know there was any hope or anything to hope for. Now I know there is. I hope I learn how to laugh like all the other kids in my Alateen group. I think I will.

Before I came to Alateen I thought I was making my mom drink alcohol. But when I came to Alateen I found out no one can make anybody else drink.

I feel sorry for my mom, but it feels good to know that her drinking isn't my fault.

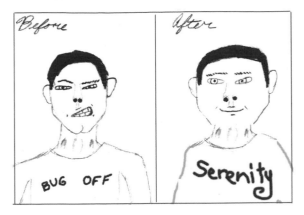

When I was very little my mother began to work in bars. This made life hard for my two brothers and me. I had to take on all of the responsibilities at home. It wasn't easy.

The little time my mom was at home was hell. I remember one day especially, because it was the day that my mom told me that she hated me. At that time I didn't know it was the alcohol doing the talking. I felt very hurt. Soon after this experience I moved out.

Now I live with my father. I attend Alateen meetings every Tuesday. In the program I have learned a lot. I've learned that it's not my fault when my parent drinks. I used to think when things went wrong that I always caused them to go wrong. Now I can see that alcoholism is a disease that affects our whole family. In Alateen I've learned to live and love again, and I've learned that I'm special too. I've learned that all of the children of alcoholics everywhere are very special.

Before I came to Alateen I heard my parents fighting a lot while I hid in the basement. My father drank all the time. My mother decided to divorce him.

When I was in the seventh grade I heard a speaker at school talk about Alateen. I was in therapy at the time. Therapy helped me stand up for myself, but it didn't help me get rid of the anger that I had toward my father.

One night I went to an Alateen meeting. It really helped.

A year later my father got worse. He lost his visitation rights, and I haven't wanted to have any more contact with him.

Thanks to Alateen and my mother, I have a life of my own to live. I'm doing well in school, and I've decided to become a journalist. In Alateen I've met a lot of new people who are just like I am.

⁂

Before I came to Alateen it seemed like I was being followed by a black cloud. I was miserable. My life was unmanageable, and I was a totally different person. I felt a constant fear that something was going to happen to my parents, or maybe even to me.

Today I'm glad that I can call and talk to someone in Alateen about my fears, my frustrations, and my problems.

⁂

Before I came to Alateen my mom and father drank. Today my father still drinks, but my mom is trying to find a new life in AA.

Now I don't have my old fear of being abandoned. I'm not worried about being left to take care of my brother all by myself. Today I'm not worried about where my parents are, or if they're even alive.

Today if I have a problem I have a place to go to or people I can call. Today I have learned different ways of showing my anger, fear, or sadness—instead of just by fighting. Today I read my Alateen book as part of my normal routine.

All of the changes in me took time. They didn't happen in

just one day, like I wanted them to. I had to think about my program and about how to work it into my life. Little by little, one day at a time, I became a better person. I'm not perfect, but I'm myself. And I must put myself first.

✍

Before I came to Alateen my life just slipped by. I didn't have a reason to live. I was just here.

The love and friendship I found in Alateen opened my eyes to a beautiful, brighter world. I know I have friends that understand my problems at home. It also makes me feel good about myself, knowing that I can help other people, too. All I have to do is the same thing everybody's been doing for me.

It works when I work it.

✍

Before I came to Alateen I felt helpless and confused. It seemed like the only thing I learned was how to pack boxes and take apart my day bed. Because of my mother's drinking we were always having to move.

Now, no matter where we move I can usually find an Alateen group. I hope Alcoholics Anonymous can help my mom.

✍

Before I came to Alateen my mom and I fought a lot. We weren't close. I held all of my feelings inside. All of the time I called her bad names in my mind.

Every time my mom yelled at me I'd run to my bedroom and slam the door. I wouldn't come out until dinner time. My dad drank a lot while all of this was going on, and most of the time he wasn't home.

Now that I'm in Alateen I'm much closer to my mom. I can understand why she was so unhappy when we were living with my dad. I can even understand why she took out some of her feelings on me. About a year ago my dad went to jail. Now he's in prison. I'm glad Alateen helped me learn how to be friends with my mom.

✍️

Before I came to Alateen I was outrageous and rude. Now I'm considerate, and people have told me I'm even a pleasure to be around.

✍️

Before Alateen, I dropped out of school. I just couldn't listen to teachers when my mind was on my parents all the time.

I was out of high school for three years. Thanks to Alateen, I'm back in school now. When I learned in Alateen that I needed to take care of myself, instead of waiting for my parents to learn how to do it, is when I started thinking about school again.

I'm doing what I have to do for myself today. I won't graduate until I'm 21 years old. But that's okay. I have faith in myself now. I can listen in my classes, instead of concentrating on the alcoholics in my life. Thanks to Alateen and Al-Anon, I'm right where I should be today. I'm learning, and I'm getting lots of help from people who really care about me.

When I first came to Alateen I felt scared. My father brought me to a meeting the same day that I came to live with him. He had been in AA for six months already.

I didn't know anyone at all. My dad introduced me to some of his friends' kids. I didn't really say much in the meetings at first. Then people started sharing what they were going through. It took a while for it to sink in, but I kept coming back.

Dad bought me a little orange book. I opened it to the first page, and it said, *Alateen—Hope for Children of Alcoholics.* Those six words said it all. There was hope for me if I worked the Twelve Steps.

Sponsors and other teens told me to get a sponsor. At first I ignored them and tried to work the Twelve Steps by myself. But that didn't work very well. So I finally got a sponsor.

Now I'm working the Twelve Steps, one at a time, and I'm getting help. Every day I keep feeling better. I'm really glad that it works.

My favorite line used to be, "Yes, but what if . . ."

I don't want to live like that anymore. I want my favorite line to be, "Yes, I will," or, "Yes, I need help."

In Alateen I've learned that no one is better than another person. And I've learned that asking for help isn't a sign of weakness. It's a sign of courage and strength.

I was absolutely terrified at my first Alateen meeting. I got there early, but I was afraid to go into the church where the meeting was going to be. Finally I gathered my courage and walked inside.

There had to be at least thirty teens sitting around tables. I guess I thought it was going to be like a lunch bunch in the cafeteria at school—boy, was I wrong.

The chairperson passed around the Twelve Steps and the Twelve Traditions for us to read, plus a daily reading. Then the chairperson asked if there were any topics or problems anyone wanted to discuss.

Someone started talking about a fight they had had with the alcoholic in their house. As I sat and listened to the boy talk, the story turned into my story. It was as if I was the one who was doing the talking.

The more I listened to everyone giving the speaker their support, the more pain I felt. Things began to sink in. In that one night I got in touch with so many of my feelings, and I let the feelings turn into knowledge about myself and my family. It hurt a lot to sit there and realize that my father and my brother weren't the only sick ones in my house. I was just as sick as they were, and I needed just as much help.

For years I had walked around saying how much I hated my brother and father for treating me the way they did. Sometimes I thought all my problems were because of them. I never stopped to think they might not mean the things they were saying to me. But in my very first Alateen meeting I learned that an alcoholic doesn't mean what he says, because he isn't the one who's really talking. It's the alcohol talking, and the alcoholic often says hateful things because that's the way he thinks about himself. Even though my first Alateen meeting made me hurt, it also made me feel better. The things I learned in that one night gave me a reason to have hope. I felt like I really wanted to live. I felt like I wanted to keep coming back so I could learn how to have a good life.

My mom, my sister, and my brother and I used to live by ourselves. Then my mom started to date this man. I thought he was pretty nice at first.

When they got married everything changed. It was a nightmare. He got my mom into drinking with him all the time. He never worked, so we lived off the money my mother made.

Then he started to hit me and my mom. I asked myself over and over why he was doing this. I hated him for what he was doing. I thought I would never be able to like him.

He and my mom split up for a few months. When he came back I thought maybe he would have changed. But things were the same as they used to be. So I decided that I needed to take some action.

I went to school and talked to the counselor. She gave me some phone numbers to call. The people I called got my stepdad to go to some meetings. Then our whole family went for counseling. Now my mom and my stepdad don't drink as much as they used to.

Today if things get out of hand, I usually stay in my room.

I'll shut the door, but I won't lock it, so nobody will get mad at me. I'll find something to read, or else I'll listen to the radio. If things get really bad, I have some friends in Alateen whom I can meet someplace to talk. Or I can even spend the night with one of them if I need to.

I always thought that if I let go of my dad, then I would lose him. Then I came to the point where I had to put this possibility to a test.

My dad was losing himself in a terribly long binge. As he kept drinking all day while lying in bed in his room, I no longer went in to cheer him up or to clean up after him. I didn't go in to try to make him eat. I didn't help him make it to the bathroom. I didn't even pick him up from the floor after he'd fallen.

Instead, I was taking good care of myself. I was telling my mom how I felt about what was happening to my dad. I was reaching out to my Alateen friends for support, and I was praying to God for His strength and guidance.

On the eighth day of my dad's binge, I went into his room. I told him how much I loved him, and I kissed him on the cheek. I didn't want to lose my dad, but I knew in my heart that I couldn't fight his disease anymore. I thought that this time he might die.

The next night my mom and I went out to dinner, and we left my dad at home alone. Both of us had always been there to pick up the pieces for him. Now both of us were practicing the principles of Al-Anon and Alateen.

I kept praying for the strength and courage to follow God's will. Even though I was afraid, my fear wasn't taking me over. By facing my fear, I actually started feeling calm.

On the tenth day of my dad's binge, he was so weak that his legs couldn't support him. He crashed to the floor on his way to the bathroom. No one was there to make everything better. He stayed on the floor for hours, feeling his pain and his loneliness. Finally, he started crying and asking for help. When help arrived, it was a team of medics and two members of AA.

My dad had reached his bottom, and by the grace of God he started his long climb toward recovery.

I said thank you prayers to my Higher Power all that night. I thanked Him for the courage, strength and insight I'd been given to keep taking good care of myself. Above all, I thanked Him for this wonderful program full of very special teenagers and a few very special adults. Alateen — thank you from the bottom of my heart.

THOUGHTS OF YOU
(For My Dad)

Thoughts of you running through my head, tears of hate fall onto my bed. Mind and heart are as one, and the relationship is as good as done.
A lasting love has now ended, and that's the opposite of what I intended. Thoughts of you race around my heart, as tears of hate tear us apart.

Mind and heart think of you, it seems that crying is all I can do.
A lasting love was never there, it seemed that you never really cared. Thoughts of you are all around my head, and tears of hate show what I said.
Mind and heart are heard no more, all is hidden behind a door.

But a lasting love is always here, in my heart I know you do care.

Before I joined Alateen I thought I didn't fit in. I always felt out of place in school. I also used to hide my feelings. I would never tell anyone how I felt, except maybe my best friend.

My mom didn't want to admit that my dad had a problem. Then she finally broke down and admitted that my dad had a problem with alcohol. When she did that I felt part of a big burden being lifted off my shoulders. I thought since Mom admitted that Dad actually had a problem then everything was going to be okay.

But everything didn't turn out okay. After a while my dad said he would go and get help, but he only went to one AA meeting. When he first told me about his decision to go to AA I was so happy. After I found out that he only went to one meeting, I hated him.

Then one day at a support group my school counselor told me about Alateen. She gave me a pass to go to one of the meetings at my school.

Now that I'm in Alateen I've learned how to open up and share my feelings. I have people to turn to who will listen when I talk. I can tell they really care about me. Finally, I feel like I really belong. I fit in.

I will always be grateful to the people in Alateen and to the counselor who helped me. I'd just like to say thank you for listening to my problems. If it wasn't for you, I'd probably still hide my feelings. I'd never really go after my dreams.

Before I came to my Alateen group I felt like my dad's drinking problem meant the end of the world for me. Fortunately, I met kids at the meeting that felt the same way I did. Although I didn't know any of them before the meeting, I got used to them right away.

I'm very happy that I joined my Alateen group.

When I was in the fourth grade I started coming to Alateen. My dad had a problem with alcohol. Alateen helped me through all of the hurts and pains in my family. Then my mother got remarried.

My stepfather likes to yell at me and call me names. When he started hitting me I asked my Alateen group for help. I don't know where I would be now if it wasn't for Alateen. Now I call Alateen my home.

Before I came to Alateen, my life was a mess. I was a loner. I didn't have many friends. I didn't have any love from my family.

My dad was always at work, and when he did come home all he'd do was yell at us, put us down, and hit us. My mom was all right to me for awhile, but eventually she ended up giving me "unwanted love." It wasn't safe, good love, if you know what I mean. And my brother and I hated each other.

As time went on, my brother started drinking, and he

became very violent. I can't tell you how many holes he put in the wall, or how many doors have been torn off hinges, or how many countless bruises I've gotten from him.

All I know is before I came to Alateen I lived with lots of fear, hopelessness, and anger. I started doing crazy things, like not eating, or eating a lot and then throwing up. I hurt myself in a lot of different ways. I have many scars that I will carry with me for the rest of my life.

Slowly, my brother's drinking got even worse, but my parents refused to believe that there was a problem. I got tired of waking up in the morning to find a bunch of trashed guys sleeping on the floor, having my money stolen, and finding things missing from my room. I got tired of having police cars at our house all the time. And I was starting to feel real tired of life.

I didn't know what to do, except to feel totally crazy. You wouldn't believe some of the things that I thought I saw or some of the things I thought I heard. At that point I was right at the end of my rope.

But then one of my friends invited me to Alateen. My parents still don't know that I go. What I found at Alateen is that I'm not alone. And I'm not going crazy. And I found love— real, safe love. I found the kind of love that makes me feel good about being myself.

I've only been going to Alateen for about six months, but I'm on my way to getting my life back together. I'm starting to take lots better care of myself. Things are still bad at home, but I'm learning to live my own life. I'm learning how to cope with my family situation. If I hadn't found Alateen I don't know what my life might be like by now. I don't know if I'd even have a life. I'm feeling very thankful.

Before_I_came_to_Alateen_I_always_got_into_trouble.__
I_always_ran_my_mouth_off.__
But_after_I_started_Alateen_I_learned_how_to_keep_
my_mouth_shut,_more_than_I_used_to.

Before Alateen I thought the only way to get my anger out was to yell, or sometimes to hit someone in my family. But after I started going to Alateen I realized that's not the way to handle it.

My first couple of meetings I mostly listened. Then, about my third or fourth time to Alateen, I spoke up. I asked other people how they handled their anger. Someone told me that they write down all of their thoughts when they feel angry. I tried that and it worked. So now whenever I get mad I write down everything I'm thinking and feeling. I've been in Alateen a long time, and to this day I still handle my anger this way. It really helps me a lot.

I was seventeen when I went to my first Alateen meeting. I'd thought for the longest time I was the only one whose mother had a drinking problem. I felt ashamed of how she behaved. I didn't know if I could talk to anyone about my life and my mom. But as soon as I started going to meetings I discovered that I wasn't alone.

I was really surprised. I found out that other members went through the same kinds of situations I did. It was like all of us had grown up together. It made me feel so much better to know I wasn't alone. I could relax and talk in Alateen meetings. I could tell people about my mom and about her alcoholism.

Six years later, I'm in Al-Anon now after spending three years in Alateen. My mom is in AA. The rest of my family is recovering too. Once in awhile I still slip back into old behaviors when I'm with my family. But I know how to detach from their problems today. I'll be working my program for a long time. When I keep coming back, I keep learning how to live my own life, one day at a time.

✍

My most painful experience was leaving both of my parents. My father is an active alcoholic, and my mom doesn't seem to want to be a part of my life.

Being in Alateen has given me support, self-confidence and, most of all, love. I was starved for love before I came into the program, and Alateen has filled that hunger.

My Alateen family is the only family that I have. I would feel lost without them.

✍

Before I came to Alateen I was always sticking my nose into other people's business. Alateen has helped me think about myself and what I'm doing, instead of always worrying about my sister or my brothers.

I'm glad to know I'm not the only one whose family has the problem of alcoholism.

✍

Before I started Alateen I was really confused. I thought something I was doing was making the alcoholic drink. I also thought there was something wrong with me because I couldn't get him to stop. I was afraid to say something to him because I was afraid he'd yell at me.

When I first came to Alateen I was nervous. I wasn't sure how I would be treated, but I was treated with love from the start. I never had a meeting where I felt that I was unwanted. I've been going to Alateen for a year and a half, and it has really helped me. My dad is still drinking, but now I know that I can't change him, can't make him stop, and can't worry about him all the time. With slogans like "Live and Let Live," I can get through it.

My sponsors have been a big help during my recovery. I've talked to them about everything from problems at home to little things like what I did at school one day. We talk a lot at our meetings about how Alateen has helped us. I know I feel better about myself and more confident.

I got in trouble not too long ago for seeing a guy my mom and dad didn't like. They told me not to see him anymore, but I saw him anyway. I told my problem at Alateen. My sponsor told me that once I told my Higher Power about it, I would feel better, and she was right. Now every time I think about being grounded I use the phrase, "I am responsible"—which means I'm responsible for my own actions and not for anyone else's. With the help of the program, my sponsors, my mom and others, and Alateen literature, I know I can get through anything.

✍

The alcoholic and I have gone our separate ways. Even so, I know that the program is leading me to be a better person. I trust it, and I am very grateful for it.

I give thanks to everyone in Alateen. You have a very special place in my heart.

✍

I was always scared to go home, because my father was violent and very impatient. When I was at school I was always worrying and scared for my mom. I couldn't concentrate on what I was doing because I couldn't think about anything else. It was the same way when I was with my friends.

But today I feel good. My father's not drinking anymore. He has time to talk to me and my mom. You wouldn't believe some of the things we say to each other. I even bring some of my friends home with me. That was impossible before Alateen.

✍

My Life

My life is like an
unpaved road.

It can be smooth,
or it can be
bumpy.

When I go down
this road and hit
the potholes,

I must have good suspension.
I must proceed to the next
smooth section.

I must learn how to pave these
roads, because I live on them.

When I was younger my biggest fear was coming home from school. I knew when I got home I'd have to deal with my drunk mother. But my even bigger fear was my friends coming home with me and seeing my mother drunk.

I remember telling some of my friends when they came over that my mother was sick. Eventually, of course, I told all of my friends the truth. Many of them, especially my Alateen friends, helped me get through those crises.

But today I'm proud and happy to have my friends come over to my house. I like them to meet my mom. She's done a lot of work on herself in AA, and I've done a lot of work on myself in Alateen. Many of my long-time friends have learned from my experiences. They've learned how alcohol can change people's lives.

Now I'm proud to show off my mom, instead of being ashamed of her.

✍

Before Alateen my life was a mess. I was at my rope's end. Thinking of suicide was an everyday thing for me. My mom and stepfather were breaking up because of alcohol among other things. And when my mom told me about Alateen I was ready to try anything. Now that I'm in Alateen I don't want to kill myself anymore. I don't even think about it since I know that isn't the way to solve my problem. I know that we are better off without my stepfather, since his drinking made our lives miserable. And I know if I keep coming back I'll keep getting the help I need. I also know that I don't have to please everybody. And the one thing I'll always keep with me is I'm never alone, never. That makes me feel good inside because I always felt like an outcast since my stepfather drank and my parents fought. But I'm not and I never have to feel that way again. Alateen also showed me to trust in believing in my higher power. Give it to him and he'll take it all away whatever it is. Thanks Alateen!

Workshop On
BEFORE AND AFTER

Complete the following sentences, adding as many sentences as you want.

Before I came to Alateen, I was ...

Before Alateen, I was worried and concerned about ...

I came to Alateen because ...

Now that I have been to Alateen I ...

I kept coming back to Alateen because ...

The ways Alateen has helped change me are ...

A FEW SPECIAL WORDS FROM ALATEEN
Including Slogans, Sayings and Al-Anon/Alateen Phrases

LET GO AND LET GOD
EASY DOES IT
Live and Let Live
How Important Is It?
Listen and Learn
First Things First
Together We Can Make It
Keep it Simple
One Day At a Time
Think

Our slogans and sayings are tools that help us get through difficult times in our lives. The slogan, **Together We Can Make It**, helps us remember that we do not have to do it all alone. The Alateen group can be an important part of our life.

Alateens share on
A FEW SPECIAL WORDS

I chose **"Just For Today"** as my favorite slogan because it helps me to cope with things, one at a time. When I wake up in the morning I think things like, "Just for today I'll try to get along with my family," or, "Just for today I'll tell my father how I actually feel." Another one is, "Just for today I'll deal with me first" (that one's real special). "Just For Today" has helped me a lot with my Alateen meetings and with my home life.

Easy Does It . . .

. . . helps me to slow down. When I'm hurrying around the house, mad at everyone, I sometimes think of this slogan, and it helps me a lot. It also helps when I'm confused about my homework or something. It reminds me that I don't have to be perfect.

EASY DOES IT . . . .

Let Go And Let God . . .

. . . really fits into my program. It helps me get rid of my resentments and fears. I feel very safe and comfortable with this slogan because I can let go of a problem and let God help me with it. It's not the same as giving up, because things can change for the better when I'm using this slogan, even though I'm not controlling what happens.

Before I started coming to Alateen, I didn't know what was going on. My father came home drunk all the time, and my mother was using drugs. Then one day my dad said something about going to an Al-Anon meeting. He asked me if I wanted to go to an Alateen meeting, so I went.

At first I totally hated it. Now I love it. If it wasn't for my Alateen group, I'd definitely be a nervous wreck. That's why I like the slogan, **Together We Can Make It**. If I was alone, I wouldn't be able to make it. Thanks to Alateen, I'm doing a lot better.

I like Easy Does It because it helps me stop worrying so much. I also like it because it keeps me from hustling through stuff like homework and activities. "Easy Does It" helps me slow down so I can enjoy life a little more.

When my parents drank alcohol I felt like I was in a dream. My whole life seemed like it was in slow motion. It really hurt me to see the things that went on between my mom and my dad. It also hurt to see what went on between my two sisters and me.

Sometimes my parents drank so much at night that when they woke up in the morning they'd still be drunk. One day when my parents got drunk my mom said she couldn't take it anymore. She grabbed me and my nine-year-old sister and my baby sister. She put us in the car, and she slammed her foot down on the gas pedal. At the end of the driveway we got into a major accident. If we didn't have our seat belts on, and if the baby wasn't strapped into her car seat, all of us would have flown right through the windshield. Our Higher Power really was with us that day.

Now my mom is working hard to get us back. She lost us when my sister and I were put in a foster home. The only one left at home is our baby sister. Alateen helped me realize that my parents have a disease. I learned the three Cs: We didn't Cause it. We can't Control it. And we can't Cure it. It's a disease.

When I came to Alateen I had a lot of anger stored deep inside of me. Any little thing would set me off on a yelling spree.

Through Alateen I learned that all those little problems added up to one very enormous problem. Then my friends in Alateen introduced me to two important slogans, **Easy Does It**, and **How Important Is It?**

Using these slogans, I learned to face each of my problems

while they are still little. That way, I never really have to deal with an enormous problem. Using these slogans has kept me out of a lot of trouble. They've also saved my sanity.

✍

Just For Today is something I use quite often. In fact, I use it just about every day. For example, today I said "I'm gonna be in a good mood." It's not that I'm not in a good mood anyway, but it puts me in an extra happy mood, just by saying it to myself. Sometimes I'll use it when someone gets me down. I'll say, "Just for today I won't let them make me unhappy." That way, I'll be in a good mood even after somebody tries to mess up my day.

✍

To me, First Things First is the slogan I think about the most. It means a lot to me, but when I see First Things First written down it doesn't look like much. I have to really think about it to discover its real meaning.

What it means to me is I have to put myself first. I have to take care of myself before anything, no matter how hectic or crazy a situation might be. I always have to remember that I'm the most important person in my life. I count.

✍

The slogan that means a lot to me, especially when I can actually do it, is **Let Go and Let God**. I don't really have too strong a belief in God so I was never used to this slogan before. But now I find when I use it, it really helps me a lot. It not only helps me to let go, but it also helps me to let someone else deal with these problems that aren't only mine. Because of this program I actually believe in my Higher Power a lot more. I think all of these slogans are useful, but I find that "Let Go and Let God" helps me the most.

. . . to me means I have to remember every day that I'm powerless over people, places, things, and even myself at times. So, in order for me to make it through the day, I have to keep everything simple.

It's like taking baby steps through my day. I don't predict things, and I don't anticipate things that will happen. If a problem arises, I handle it by taking certain steps, such as: I remind myself that I'm powerless; I call my sponsor; I turn it over to God; I pray for the best outcome. After I have taken these steps, with the help of God and my friends and my group, I can keep my life simple.

I'm not exactly sure how it works, but I'm sure glad it does.

✍

Of all the things in Alateen, the thing that has helped me the most is the **Serenity Prayer**. When my grandmother was in the hospital, everyone thought she was going to die. The doctors said she wouldn't last until the morning. I hated to think of living without her.

The only thing that helped me deal with my fear was repeating the Serenity Prayer over and over. "God, grant me the serenity to accept the things I cannot change," was the hardest part for me to think about. Today, I still have Alateen and the Serenity Prayer to help me.

✍

My favorite saying is on the "Just For Today" card. It says: "Just for today I will try to make my own decisions. I will not let other teenagers influence the way I think or feel."

Well, for me, instead of other teenagers I substituted my alcoholic father. I didn't let him influence the way I thought or felt. In fact, for me, that's what detachment means: I'm there, and I do what I have to do, but I don't let my alcoholic father influence the way I think or the way I feel. For me, that works.

✍

When I was young my older brother sexually abused me. This affected me a lot. My older brother was an alcoholic. When I came into Alateen I didn't realize how much my brother had affected me.

The slogan, **Let Go and Let God**, helped me the most. You see, when I started seeing a counselor I'd go home feeling a lot of anger and resentment toward my brother. If I Let Go and Let God, then my pain would go away. I'm very grateful to the program for helping me learn how to live a normal life, one day at a time.

Oftentimes in my life, God's will clashes with my own will. When this happens there can be only one winner. Most of the time my will is not the one that wins. A perfect example of this is when I was supposed to be at an Alateen conference and play in a baseball game at the same time. I knew that I needed to go to the conference, but I really wanted to play in the game. So what did I decide to do? Go to the game.

When I went to the game it turned out to be the worst experience of my life. There were over-throws, mental mistakes, missed catches, and a variety of other problems. The game ended with eleven errors. In addition, I accidentally offended my coach, which caused me to get pulled from the game. Strangely enough, when I finally arrived at the Alateen conference things seemed to work out okay. This experience helped me learn all about an Alateen slogan, **First Things First**. Now all I have to do is to remember to use it.

My favorite slogan, **Let Go and Let God**, tells me that I don't have to be responsible for what everyone else does. It tells me I can take care of myself and only myself. When something is bothering me and I try to control it, I don't have to struggle with it. I can let go and hand it over to God and let Him choose the direction for it.

Slogans are a very important part of the Alateen program. Sometimes, when I can't figure out which Step or Tradition to use for my problem, I look at the slogans and I've found a lot of answers.

✍

My mom is an alcoholic. It always bothered me when she drank. She wouldn't get violent or anything like that, but she got this blank look on her face. It was like she wouldn't come back to life again until she got sober. The next day, after one of her drinking spells, I'd tell her what she did. Then she'd get mad, and she wouldn't believe me.

One night my mom's boyfriend had a bottle hidden where mom wouldn't find it, but of course she found it. She got completely drunk that night. The part that really embarrassed me, and the thing that I really had to let go of, was that my best friend was at my house that night.

My mom kept after me to give her all of my money so she could buy some more alcohol. I got my friend to help me lie to my mom. We told her that I didn't have any money. Before the night was over, I ended up crying my eyes out on my best friend's shoulder. Over and over, when I was crying I kept thinking, **Let Go and Let God**.

✍

What the slogan Keep It Simple means to me is that I shouldn't let things pile up. I shouldn't make things too difficult for myself.

✍

One slogan that has really made a difference in my years in Alateen is **How Important Is It?** My father taught me how to use it. He said when he gets upset he asks himself, "On a scale from one to ten, with ten being the complete and utter destruction of the universe, how important is it?"

It's okay to be upset, as long as I realize that there are more important things. It's okay to cry and yell, remembering that in a short time I won't even remember what I was mad about. Asking myself, "How Important Is It?" keeps me from going off on the wrong person, and saying things I don't mean. It keeps me from hurting people that I love.

✍

I always got myself involved in other people's problems. I felt so weighted down, it was like I carried a ton of bricks on my back.

Every time I fought with my dad it was my fault, not the disease's. My smile was my constant cover-up. I couldn't stand the idea of other people pitying me. I even let the fights with my dad go to my head and my stomach, so I felt sick all the time.

In Alateen I learned that it's not my problem. I learned it, but I haven't quite absorbed it yet. In fact, I'm still trying to figure it out. Now, every time I get in a fight I get hurt, but

I always say the **Serenity Prayer**. Have I figured out yet that it's not my problem? I don't know. I hope so.

✍

Okay, I'm home alone. Mom gave me a couple of chores to do while she's gone. I say, "Well, I've got a couple of hours — why don't I just watch TV for a while, and then I'll do my chores."

Things are going fine until I start feeling tired. The next thing I know I'm all laid out on the couch, doing nothing and enjoying it. All of a sudden I find myself thinking, "Gee, I've wasted a lot of time!" I start thinking about the "dreaded" chores and about being grounded.

Before I know it, I hear a car door slam. Seconds later, I find myself in front of Mom. She's yelling at me for what I did wrong. Only now do I think about a slogan from my Alateen program — **First Things First**. *Maybe next time I'll remember it a little sooner.*

✍

I have a tendency to think these really big, grandiose ideas. Right away I start making huge plans about how to make my ideas become real. That's why **Keep It Simple** is a real good slogan for me. It helps me keep my feet on the ground. Sometimes it takes me a while before I remember to use the slogan. But when I use it, it really works.

✍

Before coming to Alateen I had a very bad problem with talking back. Because I talked back all the time, I got grounded all the time. When I came to Alateen I learned the slogan, **Think**. Now, before I have a chance to talk back to my parents, I ask myself, "Is it really worth it?"

✍

I work for my father at a very large company. My father is the owner, so I have one of the best positions, but working so close to my father presents a major problem. The thing that hurts me the most is when he accuses me of wrongdoing.

At the time when he accuses me I go crazy. I say to myself, "How can he think I would do something to damage the company's profits?" What I try to do at the time of the argument is to think, "Don't argue with an alcoholic, whether he's sober or not." If I can remember to do that, then the scuffle finally ends.

The Alateen slogan that helps me remember this is **Let Go and Let God**. I could just sit there and get very mad at my dad, but I know that doesn't work. All it does is it makes me feel terrible. I know I didn't do what he accused me of, so I just let go of him yelling at me. When I let go of his anger, I can still love him. From the second that I let go of his anger, I can start to feel good about the rest of my day at work.

✍

There are a lot of slogans that I like, but my favorite probably would be "Live and Let Live" because I can apply it to my life more than the rest. "Live and Let Live" is such a beautiful slogan. I picked it as my favorite because I finally realized that I am a beautiful person.

✍

In my life I've gone through many hardships. After conquering these hardships I've gained experience, strength, and hope. I've also gained many responsibilities. I often take on too many responsibilities, and I find myself overworked to the point of exhaustion. When I catch myself doing this, I stop and think, **Let Go and Let God**." Then I'll say the Serenity Prayer until I'm at peace with myself. "Let Go and Let God" helps me let go of my problems and my worries. Most of all, "Let Go and Let God" gives me a chance to take care of myself.

✍

I was far from home on my vacation and desperately in need of a meeting. Luckily, I'd planned ahead and I'd gotten the times and dates of some of the meetings in nearby towns. I left really early so I could be sure to find the right place, but I was really nervous.

I wondered how I would fit in. I wondered if the meeting would be anything like my home meeting. I guess it's always scary for me going somewhere new, trying something new, or reaching out to others. Well, I found the town and the street. I parked the car. I walked down the street and I noticed there were just storefronts and a couple of bars. I was sure I was in the wrong place.

I felt very afraid and very lonely. Between two stores was a small alley. I felt really scared, but I saw a light above a doorway in the alley. I cautiously walked up to the door where there was a sticker that said, "EZ DUZ IT." I was so nervous that I didn't make the connection until I'd gone halfway up the stairs.

Of course, the slogan was there to let me know that I'd found my meeting. I did fit in. Even though there were different faces, the program worked the same as it does in my home group meeting. If I could just remember **Easy Does It** more often, I'd save myself a lot of worrying.

✍

My very worst experience was when my dad died. I thought it was all my fault because I wasn't there to stop him. If I could change anything in this whole wide world, it would be for my father to come back and never pick up a drink again. It really hurt me that I couldn't change that.

It took Alateen and the **Serenity Prayer** to teach me how to accept the things that I can't change. That means that

I can forgive myself for not saving my dad. It wasn't my fault, and it's not right for me to go on punishing myself for something that I didn't do. God, grant me the courage to change the things I can. Help me to find the courage to be good to myself.

✍

When I first started Alateen I had a short temper. Any little thing would send me into a fit. My big helpers in Alateen were two slogans, **How Important Is It?** and **Think**. Both of these slogans would run through my mind before I lost my temper. They kept me out of a lot of trouble.

✍

When I was younger I tried to fix everything by myself. I thought I could do it all. Even when my friends had a problem, I was their counselor.

Then I started Alateen. I started putting my own needs first. I really felt selfish. I felt embarrassed because I was so selfish. But lately I've been hearing a new slogan, **Let It Begin with Me**. This new slogan helps me realize that unless I take real good care of myself, I won't be able to help anyone else.

✍

When I first came to Alateen I didn't like the **Serenity Prayer**. The words meant different things to me then. God, grant me the serenity, meant just a big question — What is serenity? To accept the things I cannot change, meant I didn't need to change anything. The courage to change the things I

can, and the wisdom to know the difference, made me think—
Is this line saying I'm stupid and that I have no guts?

It's amazing what a change of attitude can do. Today, God, grant me the serenity, means asking God to give me peace of mind. To accept the things I cannot change, means help me to know my limitations. The courage to change the things I can and wisdom to know the difference means for me to be brave enough and clear-headed enough to tell which is which.

✍

When things get really tough at home, I can't take it all in. I have to take it One Day At A Time. School is the same way. When my teacher starts hassling me or when my grades drop, sometimes I have to take it minute by minute.

✍

To me, **Let Go and Let God** doesn't mean to forget about something. It means to relieve myself of a burden. The burden is still there, but God is carrying it.

✍

When I first started coming to Alateen meetings, I always heard the old-timers talking about something called serenity. They always said how much serenity they had after a meeting. Being new, I wasn't too sure what they meant. I thought serene meant not doing anything about your problems, just forgetting about them and living in a fantasy world.

For years, I had seen the alcoholics in my family sitting around the house saying, "Isn't this great?— I'm not doing anything, and I like it. This is happiness, peacefulness," — as they finished off another can of beer and threw it towards the garbage, missing every shot. Why would I want to be like them? I came to Alateen to get away from that kind of behavior.

Well, I stuck with the meetings, and each time I went back I learned a little bit more about serenity. Now I know that serenity is a feeling inside of myself that's calm and content. It has nothing to do with not dealing with my problems. It has something to do with not dealing with other people's problems for them. To be serene isn't to be out of touch with reality. It has to do with being in touch with my own needs.

Serenity is taking care of myself, getting done what needs to be done, and living my life in a positive way. Without the program, I wouldn't have learned what serenity really is. And I wouldn't have been able to receive that little bit of serenity that I feel each time I go to an Alateen meeting.

Workshop On
SLOGANS, SAYINGS AND PHRASES

Complete the following sentences, adding as many sentences as you want.

My favorite slogan is ...

To me this slogan means ...

A saying or phrase that has helped me is ...

To me this saying or phrase means ...

INTRODUCTION TO THE TWELVE STEPS OF ALATEEN

The Twelve Steps can be a way of life for each of us in Alateen — a full, rich, happy way of life.

At first we might think that the Steps don't really apply to us. But if we really want to build a better life for ourselves, then each Step can help us get a little closer to where we want to go.

For some of us the easiest part is admitting that we are powerless over alcohol and that our lives have become unmanageable. For others, the easiest part might be believing in a Higher Power, or making a decision to turn our will and lives over to the care of our Higher Power. What's easy for one of us might be very difficult for someone else.

Of course, what seems especially difficult for a lot of us is anything that makes us feel afraid. That's where the Twelve Steps are especially valuable. No matter what we're afraid of, the Twelve Steps can help. They offer us a way to face our fears, a little bit at a time, so that we can build our courage. They offer us a way to take very good care of ourselves, even if no one else is taking care of us right now.

Sometimes we feel tempted to skip some of the Steps. If a lot of our pain has gone away, then we think we're finished, but we are not finished just because we don't feel bad anymore. The pain will surely return, but the Steps offer us a positive way to face our feelings with courage and strength. If we stop after working just a few of the Steps, then we will never know how good we can feel when we work through all of them.

The Twelve Steps can give everyone a full, rich, happy way of life. All we have to do is work them.

ALATEEN'S TWELVE STEPS

1. We admitted we were powerless over alcohol—that our lives had become unmanageable.
2. Came to believe that a Power greater than ourselves could restore us to sanity.
3. Made a decision to turn our will and our lives over to the care of God *as we understood Him*.
4. Made a searching and fearless moral inventory of ourselves.
5. Admitted to God, to ourselves and to another human being the exact nature of our wrongs.
6. Were entirely ready to have God remove all these defects of character.
7. Humbly asked Him to remove our shortcomings.
8. Made a list of all persons we had harmed, and became willing to make amends to them all.
9. Made direct amends to such people wherever possible, except when to do so would injure them or others.
10. Continued to take personal inventory and when we were wrong promptly admitted it.
11. Sought through prayer and meditation to improve our conscious contact with God *as we understood Him*, praying only for knowledge of His will for us and the power to carry that out.
12. Having had a spiritual awakening as the result of these Steps, we tried to carry this message to others, and to practice these principles in all our affairs.

Alateens share on
THE TWELVE STEPS IN GENERAL

As a new Alateen member I was very intimidated by the Twelve Steps. I figured the "easier" tools of the program were for the Alateens and the "sophisticated" materials (such as the Steps) were directed toward the adults in Al-Anon. I often read the Steps, but words such as "God," "searching, and fearless moral inventory," "prayer," "meditation" and "having had a spiritual awakening" frightened me away.

I convinced myself I wasn't ready and that I was afraid of God. What would happen if I made a searching inventory and I hated ME? I'd had enough rejection in my life; but if I rejected myself, then there wouldn't be anybody left to be on my side. I prayed, but meditation was too deep for me. What would happen if I tried to have a spiritual awakening and failed?

After three years of making up excuses, I realized two things. First, it's better to have tried and failed than not to have tried at all and second, keep it simple. So guess what happened? I did it!

1. I had nothing to do with my father's drinking and my life was certainly a wreck.

2. I needed someone, and I chose to turn to God and Alateen because I couldn't do it alone.

3. In the beginning, when my father's drinking was active, I associated his personality with God's—both seemed angry and unforgiving. Today, my God is a loving god, and no matter what I do, He will always forgive me.

4. I took a piece of paper and listed all of the negative and positive aspects of my character. For each negative defect, I listed something positive.

'red this Step with my Alateen sponsor as well as my ,gher Power and myself.

ɔ & 7. Steps Six and Seven are a daily part of my life. I know all of my shortcomings and they don't disappear overnight. If I feel impatient, at that moment I ask God for patience.

8. This Step was easy, it was preparation for Step Nine. I made a list of people I had hurt.

9. This Step was more difficult. I might have been rejected, and the people I hurt might not have accepted my apologies. I had to remember that if I was doing this for myself and nobody else, then I'd have the courage to accomplish Step Nine. I couldn't believe how much healthier I felt about myself and how full my heart felt, just from trying Step Nine.

10. This Step is difficult only if I don't practice it daily, because things tend to build up. I have to throw away my pride; because it only gets in the way. The more I live Step Ten, the more I become the real me.

11. I found out that prayer and meditation aren't quite the same. God is my friend. In my prayers I can talk to Him. I can ask Him for knowledge of His will for me and the power to carry it out. On the other hand, in my meditations I try to quiet myself enough to let God do the talking. My task in my meditations is to listen as best I can to what my Higher Power would like me to hear. Whether I'm praying or meditating, I'm trying to open myself to changes in me, rather than spending all of my energies trying to make the rest of the world do the changing.

12. Spiritually, I am awakening after completing these Steps. I feel refreshed, as though I have just completed a much-needed rest. I feel a huge sense of relief. I feel very re-

laxed. I feel closer to God and to myself. I feel so good about myself and about my place in the world that I want to carry the Alateen message of recovery to everyone who wants it and needs it.

I wish there was some way that I could let everyone know that they don't need to be afraid to take these Steps. I wish someone would have convinced me a long time ago that it isn't necessary to keep waiting and waiting. The Twelve Steps are so simple, even though sometimes they aren't easy. But they are a beautiful way of life.

Alateen isn't just a place where I can unload my troubles and feel sorry for myself. Sometimes when I complain too much about my troubles it only makes them seem bigger. I can share my experiences at a meeting, but I never want to hog the whole show.

I need to use the Steps of Alateen to work the program. I came to Alateen to get rid of self-pity and resentment, not to increase their power to make me absolutely miserable. So I want to learn from others and see how they handle their lives. I want to learn from their experiences. A member once said: "The Twelve Steps were designed for desperate people (like me and my family) as a shortcut to God."

The way I speak often tells more about me than what I say. I really have to try to live the program through the Twelve Steps before I can enjoy any of the serenity that I pray for at every meeting.

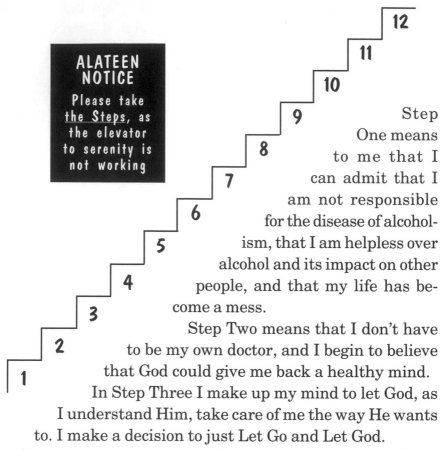

ALATEEN NOTICE

Please take the Steps, as the elevator to serenity is not working

Step One means to me that I can admit that I am not responsible for the disease of alcoholism, that I am helpless over alcohol and its impact on other people, and that my life has become a mess.

Step Two means that I don't have to be my own doctor, and I begin to believe that God could give me back a healthy mind.

In Step Three I make up my mind to let God, as I understand Him, take care of me the way He wants to. I make a decision to just Let Go and Let God.

Step Four meant that I decide to look into myself without fear, and to do so honestly. I make one list of all of the good things about myself and another list of all the things that are keeping me from becoming a better person than I am at the moment.

In Step Five I admit where I have been wrong — spiritually, mentally and physically. I pray about, think about, and talk to another person about my behaviors. I include the lists that I have written during my Fourth Step.

I decide with Step Six that I want to become a better person by letting go of the bad things that are on my list. I know that God helps me when I become willing.

Step Seven means to quietly ask God to show me myself; asking Him to take away those bad things that I listed in Step Four, so I can become the kind of person that God wants me to be.

Step Eight means accepting myself and wanting to apologize to those I have harmed. In making a list of people I've hurt by things I've done or said, I hope that I can be friends with them again.

With Step Nine I actually say I'm sorry to myself and to the people on my Eighth Step list. If my apology will only make matters worse for those people or for someone else, then I confine my apologies to myself. But from that moment on, I try my best to improve the way I conduct myself.

Step Ten means that I watch myself. When I'm wrong I need to say so. It also means that I can add to the two lists I started in Step Four and Step Eight. Depending on what I find out about myself, I can do Steps Five, Six, Seven, Eight and Nine again.

To me, Step Eleven means trying to get closer to God by praying, thinking, and asking Him to let me know what He wants me to do. Every day I ask Him to give me the strength to carry out His will in my life.

The Twelfth Step shows me that when I realize that my life is better, then the way I carry the message to others means more than just words. Somehow, the changes that have happened to me tell others that they can have better lives too. I continue working the Steps so they'll keep helping me in my daily life.

When I came to Alateen I thought I knew how to work the program. My parents had been attending meetings for many years. I started attending meetings regularly, and I began to try to open myself up so I could share. At first things got a little bit better, but then they just stopped.

I knew something was missing from my program. Then, several months after starting the Alateen program, I heard a member speak about sponsorship and the Twelve Steps and about her Higher Power. At that time I didn't have any of those things in my life.

The very next day after I heard her speak I got a sponsor. My sponsor started helping me learn how to work the Twelve Steps. By staying in close touch with my sponsor and by working the Twelve Steps of Alateen, I found my Higher Power. Before getting a sponsor and working the Steps and before I found my Higher Power, all I was doing at meetings was complaining. I complained about everything that ever went wrong or ever could go wrong in my life. I took up a lot of time, and I probably discouraged a lot of other Alateens. I hope I didn't scare too many of them away. But now I can share from the bottom of my heart how working the Twelve Steps in the Alateen program has changed my life. You'll probably hear a lot of people say this but, believe me, this is the truth. If Alateen can work for me, it can work for anyone. I hope everyone digs in and gives it and themselves a chance.

When we first enter Alateen, many of us are very anxious to find serenity, so we hurry through our recovery. Some of us are just that way. Other members work through the program slowly and stay to help others, carrying the message and explaining how they found hope and serenity.

STEP ONE

We admitted we were powerless over alcohol — that our lives had become unmanageable.

Before any of us ever heard of Alateen we felt the pain. The pain told us that something was terribly wrong. Some of us blamed ourselves for feeling this way. Some of us blamed our parents or other relatives, or we blamed our friends. Some of us had no idea what was going on, because we felt so confused and so alone. We even tried to fool ourselves into thinking that we didn't feel hurt. By refusing to feel the pain, a lot of us tried to pretend that everything was okay.

No matter what we did on our own, we still felt bad. Finally, either we started to punish other people for our problems or we punished ourselves, or both.

The First Step in Alateen shows us what worked for those who came to Alateen before we did. It suggests that we go ahead and tell the truth about what has happened in our lives and about how we feel.

When we admit how powerless we are over the disease of alcoholism and how mixed up our lives have become, our feelings begin to change. Accepting that alcoholism is a disease helps us feel better about ourselves and our relatives and our

friends. We did not cause anyone else's disease, and neither did they. Alcoholism is just a disease.

Alateens share on
STEP ONE

When I first came to Alateen I tried to control the alcoholics in my family. I tried making them obey me, like I was their owner. But it never worked when I told them not to drink. In Alateen. I learned that I was powerless over my parents' drinking. I learned that until they wanted to quit, no one could make them quit.

I don't try to boss my parents around anymore. With the help of the program, I'm accepting them for who they are. My parents are active alcoholics. I hope they get better, but for right now they're doing all the things that active alcoholics do.

I just need to keep coming to Alateen meetings, so I can keep learning how to take care of myself.

✐

When I found out that my brother was an alcoholic, I blamed myself for it. But by coming to Alateen I've learned that my brother has a disease.

Some of the things that used to go on at my house were crazy. Like the day my father was arrested for drunk driving. He made a big point of telling me how much he was going to make me trust him again. He was going to do right by me.

Right. So what happened that same night? That same night we got another call from the police. They said they needed my mother and me to come and get my dad because he was drunk. I felt so hurt that night. It took away all my hopes for my father's recovery. It felt like it was the worst day of my life.

It took Alateen to put my life in better perspective than I could. Alateen taught me that it isn't a good idea to let an active alcoholic affect me so much. It would be better for me to focus on my own life, instead of on my dad's.

Alateen taught me that my father will stop drinking if and when he is ready to stop.

✍

Of all the Steps, I've had the most experience with the First Step. I like to substitute other things I'm having trouble with, besides alcohol. For example... I'm powerless over my sister. Or... I'm powerless over my teacher.

I had a lot of guilty feelings before I started in Alateen. Now that I've been in the program for a few years, I've learned that a lot of those things that I felt guilty about were not things that I did wrong. They weren't even my responsibility in the first place. It wasn't so much that my life felt unmanageable, my life really was unmanageable.

✍

I just started coming to Alateen. After all of the darkness and pain in my life, I have a feeling inside that there's finally going to be a light at the end of the tunnel for me.

To tell you a little about myself, my real dad and mom are alcoholics. When I was seven years old, my dad hit bottom, and he just couldn't handle it. Instead of getting help, he took his own life.

My mom, however, is still drinking and living with an active alcoholic.

For me, each time I go to Alateen the pain seems to go away, little by little. I'm learning to accept the things I cannot change and to live one day at a time.

Thanks for giving me hope.

✍

This is my first time here. I came to Alateen today because I have an alcoholic father, and I need help.

✍

When I was little I was abused by both of my alcoholic parents. I especially suffered from being yelled at all day by my alcoholic mom. I remember when she had company at our house she would try to impress her friends by kicking us out of the house.

When I became a teenager I would leave home when she was intoxicated. Then I'd usually get into some kind of trouble. Most of the time I just wouldn't come home until I knew she was already asleep.

But now I've moved into a home with a family that doesn't suffer from alcoholism. I really feel safe.

Also, I just started attending Alateen meetings. The Alateens are helping me learn how to share my feelings because I feel safe there, too.

I guess my whole life is starting to change, because of how safe I'm feeling. It's really new to me and I like it.

✍

My dad drinks a lot. He says he does not have a disease and that he does not need AA. I've tried to tell him he's wrong, but he won't listen to me.

When I found Alateen I changed myself. I learned that I can't change my father, and I learned that he'll do whatever he wants to do.

Maybe someday he'll want to feel better.

✍

I thought my dad was crazy. I would pour out his beer when he was drinking. He would never listen to me. He verbally and mentally abused me. He called me names, and he blamed me for things I didn't do. He slept three-quarters of the time, and the rest of the time he was screaming at me.

He didn't seem to be very interested in the things that were important to me. He wouldn't go outside and play catch or practice soccer with me. We wasted a lot of years arguing and screaming at each other.

Now my dad has stopped drinking, and he goes to AA meetings. My mom goes to Al-Anon, and my brother and I go to Alateen. Since alcoholism is a family disease, it's nice that we can all go to the same place to get the different kinds of help that we need.

Now my father and I do more father-son things together, like fishing and talking. I think this is because I've been going to Alateen twice a week for about two months. I hope my father and I will do a lot more things together in the future.

When I finally got a sponsor, after three years of members telling me to get one, I really didn't know what to expect. I wanted my sponsor to tell me what to do and how to feel. But every time I approached her with a problem all she would say was, "It's okay." Or she'd say, "You're okay." These simple words that she shared with me were very frustrating. I was interpreting them to mean, "Oh, poor baby, it'll be okay."

I didn't feel very good about what I was hearing. After a few talks with her, I finally asked her, "What do you think this is doing for me? You're telling me it's okay, but it's not okay . It's terrible! You tell me I'll be okay, but I just get more depressed."

She said, " I mean my words in a very matter-of-fact way, not to comfort you, but to confront you. These words can give you an opportunity to accept what's happening in your life. After you accept the truth, then you can move on."

I sat in silence as I absorbed the wisdom she was trying to give to me. She was trying to give me a choice. I could accept and move on, or I could stay stuck and dwell on the worst possible interpretation of what was going wrong in my life at that moment. The choice was up to me. My first sponsor didn't tell me what to do. She left me in charge of my own life.

Now that I'm sponsoring people too, I try to let them know that everything is okay, just the way it is. I try not to run their lives, just like my sponsor didn't run mine. I try to let them discover that they have choices.

I wanted to fit in with my father. Being an only child, I had no brothers or sisters to talk with, and other kids didn't understand what was happening to me. This made me believe that the problem was me.

I remember crying for hours. I remember talking to God, asking Him to take me out of this world. I felt so worthless and miserable because nothing seemed to work.

It seemed like the only time my father and I got along was when he was drunk. So I tried to become one of my dad's drinking buddies. I had my own stein for kegs. I drank beer, despite the terrible taste. I did it because I liked hearing someone at parties say, "He's so cute." I especially liked it when my dad introduced me as, "his kid."

Then one day my dad got arrested driving his car while he was drunk. He decided to quit drinking, and I became lost. When he quit drinking he started taking drugs like crack-cocaine and heroin. For the next couple of years our lives were really bad.

My parents fought a lot. My own feelings went up and down all the time when my dad was in and out of jail so much.

I remember wanting to turn to drugs, the way I did with alcohol, so I could be accepted by my father. But I didn't want my life and my health to be like his.

I felt completely confused. I both loved and hated my dad. Finally, one day something happened that started to make my life better.

I came home from school to find my dad and his friend snorting cocaine. My father looked right at me, and he asked me if I wanted some. So this was my chance, the one that I thought I wanted. I could become my father's buddy again. But I said no. And my father's next remark was, "You're a smart kid."

My dad had tears in his eyes when he said this to me. I'll always remember the way he looked. My feelings were going crazy, all mixed up, but really strong.

Suddenly I realized that my dad loved me but that he was real sick. I didn't hate him anymore, and I didn't hate myself. I think it was a valuable lesson that I learned from my father that day. He went to jail two more times, and a judge recommended that I should go to Alateen.

I realize that not everyone's story has a happy ending, but mine does. I've been in Alateen for over five years. My best friend is in Alateen. He's like the brother I never had. I've done a lot of crying and talking and listening in Alateen. It's okay. I'm okay. And my dad is clean and sober today.

Before I joined Alateen I tried to punish alcoholics in my family by telling them that I hated them. Then I'd run away. When these punishments didn't work I felt unloved and frustrated.

Because I was the caretaker, I constantly felt as though everything was my fault or my responsibility. I'd call in sick for my father, mediate my parents' fights, and apologize for my dad's tantrums.

When my punishments weren't leading to any changes, I felt like I just wasn't trying hard enough. I think my main problem wasn't my resentment toward my parents, I think it was my overwhelming sense of powerlessness. I wanted to be perfect, and I wanted to be around perfect people.

In Alateen I'm learning to forgive myself for not having control over my parents' actions. I'm learning to stop punishing and to start accepting.

Before Alateen, I had a hard time coping with the mistakes I made. I felt like everything I did had to be perfect. And after a while I thought I was perfect.

I couldn't find one single fault in myself, but only in others. This caused me to lose a lot of close friendships. For me, making a mistake was like hitting the lottery. It just didn't happen.

If it did happen, I was not very happy. I felt like the more mistakes I made, the more my mother would drink. It took a long time for me to realize that no matter what I did, it wasn't going to stop my mother from drinking. In Alateen I've learned that the only person I can really change is me.

Workshop On
STEP ONE

**We admitted we were powerless over alcohol—
that our lives had become unmanageable.**

**Complete the following sentences, adding as many
sentences as you want.**

When I admit I am powerless over alcohol, I realize ...

Something that causes me to feel powerless is ...

My life is unmanageable when ...

When I admit that my life is unmanageable, I am ...

It is important for me to admit that my life is unmanageable because ...

I admit my life is unmanageable by ...

I become willing by ...

STEP TWO

**Came to believe that a power greater than ourselves
could restore us to sanity.**

When we blamed ourselves or other people for someone
having the disease of alcoholism, we were not thinking as
well as we could. When we began to understand how the
disease affected not only the drinker but also us, we started
to think more clearly again.

There are many things that are more powerful than we
are in this world. What this really means is that we are not in
charge. By accepting how limited our power is we can begin
to make it easier on ourselves and the people around us.

Sanity carries with it a feeling of calmness. For some of
us, being restored to sanity means getting in touch with what
it is like to feel calm again. Music, friendship, love, our Alateen
group, God—all have more than enough power to help us be
calm. Hearing how a Higher Power helped others gives us
hope that our Higher Power could do the same for us.

I know there's a power greater than myself. My mom and my counselor keep telling me that there is no problem in life that I can't get through. I also have brothers and sisters who have always been there for me.

I guess I'm lucky when I realize all the help I've been given in my life. The most recent source of real support has come from my Alateen group.

For some people, God is a major source of help and comfort. He is for my mother, but I find it hard to talk to someone that I can't see. Maybe I'm just not ready to accept Him into my life yet.

✍

When I first went to Alateen I was very scared. I thought the people in the Alateen meeting were going to make fun of my problems. But I was wrong.

The people in the meeting treated me better than I'm used to treating myself. They listened while I cried. They nodded their heads and agreed with me when I talked. I felt something come back inside of me that's been gone for a long time.

I keep coming back because I like the way the program helps me to feel good about myself. If I don't love myself, I'll be missing out on something really good.

The members and the sponsor in my Alateen group are doing something for me that I couldn't do for myself. They make me feel loved without me having to do anything to earn it.

✍

I came to Alateen because I have an alcoholic parent, and I need sanity.

✍️

Alateen is helping me understand a lot of feelings that I've had. My alcoholic father would abuse my mother or my brother or my sister. I felt very hurt because he didn't beat me as much as he beat everybody else. I really thought the reason for not beating me was because he didn't love me as much as he loved them.

Since then, my thinking has changed a lot. Now it really hurts me to remember one of my family members screaming or crying because of something my father was doing to them.

I'm learning how to deal with my feelings. I feel safe in my group. The meetings are helping me open my mind and my heart to get out the things that are buried deep inside of me. It's taking me a long time, but I'm getting there.

✍️

Growing up, I felt like a rag doll. Every week my brother and I went to my father's house. The routine was always the same. On the way to his house after dinner in a restaurant he would always stop to pick up a bottle of "medicine." That's what he called alcohol. Then we'd watch a video, usually a horror show. If I didn't like the movie, then I could watch TV in the other room.

If my brother or I said the wrong thing to my father, my father would say, "If you don't get that look off your face, I'm going to hit you so hard you'll wish you never had that face!"

I always felt more sorry for my brother than I did for myself. I was more assertive and strong-willed. My brother was shy and lacked self-confidence. My dad picked on him more than he did on me.

I remember staring at my father with my jaw hard, because I refused to give him the satisfaction of seeing me cry or fear him. I didn't let him know, but one of the things that really bothered me was when he said, "You know, I'm strong enough to throw you out the window!"

I hated the way my father always made us so scared. Also, I hated the way it affected me. I found myself yelling at people when I felt angry, the same way my father did. It wasn't right, but I couldn't stop it. I hated my life. I hated my loneliness. I hated me.

I can still feel angry about those things, but something about me is changing. The other day my father called. When I answered and realized it was him, I didn't want to be angry at him anymore. It scared me because I really don't want to trust him, either.

My feelings for my father are weird. It's even crossed my mind that someday we might have a normal father-daughter relationship. In the meantime, I'm looking out for what's best for me, and I'm learning to respect myself.

Alateen has helped me face the truth about what has been happening in my life. It has also given me the support that I need from people who have been through the same things I'm going through. It's giving me hope that somehow everything's going to be okay.

Alateen opened my mind to the idea that I have a Higher Power. I always believed in God, but I never thought that He would help me.

I may never understand why my father drinks, but at least I can count on someone always being there for me—my Higher Power.

***

In the beginning I didn't think Alateen was anything special. I was one who had been "sent" to Alateen for three months by my parents.

I served my sentence. During this time I learned many valuable things, although I wasn't realizing it.

I stopped going for three months. It was the same amount of time that my sentence had been. In this time I tried suicide on three different occasions.

Today I'm very glad that I didn't succeed. I finally realize why my life was so miserable. I came back to Alateen, and now I'm celebrating four years in the program.

I'm still alive. I'm enjoying myself, and I have a future. Although I live life one day at a time, I can't help wondering if I would still be alive if it wasn't for Alateen and the valuable friends I have made here.

***

Alateen has helped me grow mentally, emotionally, and physically. I say physically because since Alateen my self-esteem has grown so much that I don't want to hurt myself anymore. I remember I didn't eat very well. I didn't get enough sleep. I never took vitamins.

No wonder I feel good about going to Alateen. It's like learning how to become a human being again.

It feels so good just spending time with people who want me to take good care of myself. I feel like these people I never met before are loving me just for being me. I don't know what my life would be like right now if it wasn't for Alateen. I hope I never have to find out.

✍

I always thought every name my father called me was true. Somehow it always seemed to fit me, until one day he called me a loser.

I got real upset. I got so upset that I called my Alateen sponsor. She said, "If he called you a chair, would that make you a chair?"

I said, "No!"

Things started to make sense to me after that. I started to realize that whatever name my dad called me didn't make it true. I felt really happy that day.

I know it probably seems like a small thing, my dad calling me names. But it felt really big at the time. Alateen does that. It takes something crazy, and it makes it make sense.

✍

Before I came to Alateen, I felt lonely and frustrated and scared. My dad never seemed to drink a lot. It's just that if he was drinking, then he was mean. If he wasn't drinking, then he was still mean. When I got into the program I learned how to deal with my problems. I know it would be harder for me, though, if I didn't have a Higher Power.

Once I had a dream that God was standing at the top of a mountain. I had a question to ask Him. I ran to Him but I couldn't reach Him. I questioned Him about it. I said, "God, why can't I reach You?" He said, "Because I'm inside of you."

Throughout my whole life I've felt cheated. I felt cheated out of all the things my friends had—like perfect families and perfect lives and perfect parents. I felt like there was something huge and horrible that I'd done to make my father want to drink all the time.

In Alateen I learned that I didn't do anything to make my father drink. I also learned that I wasn't cheated out of anything, and that my family's problems were caused by a disease called alcoholism.

I came to believe that I am loved by my parents and that I have friends who care about me. I learned that there isn't such a thing as a perfect family.

I'm grateful to Alateen for letting me discover how much my family means to me. I'm grateful for the tools it has given me to feel good about myself. My life isn't perfect, but it's mine. Today I have a life, thanks to Alateen.

In the beginning my Higher Power wasn't God. But, as Step Two says, I did believe in something greater than myself.

I had long conversations with my Higher Power. As time went on, I felt better and better. Without realizing it, I started talking to my Higher Power as if He was God.

Now my Higher Power is God.

✍

I've realized through the program that love is important. I used to believe that no one could love me. I thought that no one would ever want to love me. I hated myself and the whole world around me. Life just seemed so crazy.

After a lot of talking about my feelings and after a lot of praying to my Higher Power, I began to see how I might be lovable. Alateen showed me that people could love me and care about me, but I'd never had that experience before. It was hard for me to accept it.

Then I started to learn how to accept the love that others had for me. I learned about unconditional love. I learned that people can love you no matter what you do.

Alateen has taken away the big crazy part of my life, and I want to thank everyone in Alateen for making the world a much nicer place for me.

✍

When I was younger my father was always drinking around me. I didn't realize that he had a problem, even though a few times he gave me a drink of his beer.

It wasn't until four years ago at an Alateen meeting that I started talking about everything that was going on with me and my dad. I got some good ideas from my group.

Now I don't see my dad as much as I did before. I stopped riding in the car with him because it wasn't safe for me. I always got scared, but I didn't really understand that I could do something to help myself until I started talking about it at my Alateen meeting.

I still worry about my dad having an accident and maybe getting killed, or maybe killing somebody else. But I don't have to worry about me being the one who gets killed in his car.

I hope my dad gets help, but I won't take those kinds of chances with my life anymore.

✍

When I got to Step Two, I thought, "Well, here's a step I can skip — I haven't done anything crazy like my parents." Then as I listened to other Alateens share, I realized that I'm not immune to doing crazy things, just because I'm young. It was when I was sharing my experience, strength and hope with a newcomer that I first realized how my obsession with my dad's drinking made me do things that were not sane. Listening to myself made it easier for me to do Step Two.

I shared how one night I tried to empty my dad's bottle of booze that he had been trying to hide. I was so mad I started lecturing him—reversing the roles—acting more like a mother talking to her son, than a daughter trying to protect her father.

My insanity made me want to hurt my dad. I wanted to punch him in the arm and shake him up. But my fear of him being so big and strong stopped me. Besides, I knew that if I hit him, he wouldn't feel a thing — it would just be like a feather tickling him.

My focus on my dad made me lose my sanity. It was Alateen that helped me come to believe that I needed my Higher Power to restore whatever little sanity I had left. Today, my mom is in Al-Anon, my dad is in AA, and I've made my transition from Alateen to Al-Anon. I'm still attached to my Alateen friends, and I'm also an Alateen sponsor. Only my Higher Power knows where I'd be today if it wasn't for Alateen.

Workshop On
STEP TWO

Came to believe that a Power greater than ourselves could restore us to sanity.

Complete the following sentences, adding as many sentences as you want.

My Higher Power is ...

When I believe there is a Power greater than I am, I ...

When I believe that my Higher Power can restore me to sanity, I ...

I allow my Higher Power to restore me to sanity by ...

STEP THREE

Made a decision to turn our will and our lives over to the care of God as we understood Him.

Step Three offers us a simple way to take away a lot of our fear. All we have to do is make a decision. When we decide to let a power greater than ourselves be in charge of our lives, we do not have to know all the answers. No matter who or what we choose as our Higher Power, we do not have to be terrified of making a mistake, either.

Some of us make this same decision, to turn our will and our lives over to the care of God as we understood Him, several times every day. It is not because we think God has forgotten us; it is because we are the ones who forget. Besides, it can feel good every time we invite our God to help us in our day-to-day lives. When we feel a lot of fear it is usually because we have forgotten how much our Higher Power can help us. All we have to do is make a decision, and we can make this decision as many times as we want and as often as we want.

I try to take life one day at a time while I'm learning how to trust God. Some days I trust Him, and some days I don't.

I used to worry so much that it was hard for me to believe that everything was going to be okay. I even worried about things that never happened.

My mom and dad talked me into coming to Alateen. At first I didn't like it because the kids in my group were a lot older than I was. But I found another group that's exactly the right age for me.

Today, I've decided to trust God and my new group.

✍

I used to worry about everything. I worried about whether I would do well in school. I worried about whether people would make fun of me. I worried about whether I'd have to deal with my dad if he came home drunk after work.

Today I trust that God will take care of me and my day. I know that everything will work out.

That's what my Higher Power is for.

✍

I never really considered God as a very major power in my life until just recently. I pray almost every night before I go to bed, whenever I have problems or need help. For the past year I've been praying a lot.

I had a "best friend" who, I thought, was the only person in my life who really cared about me. People told me he was no good for me. But I cared about him, so I didn't believe what anyone told me.

Attaching to him so much and so fast was probably the worst thing I could have done. I knew fairly soon that he was very confused inside. I knew he was afraid to show his emotions. I wanted to tell him that, but I was afraid that I would lose him.

Now, a year later, I've told him what I thought and how I felt. So he says he doesn't want to have anything to do with me.

I had to get away from him, and I'm going to Alateen. I've decided to turn my will and my life over to the care of my Higher Power.

✍

I had trouble working Step Three because I never took responsibility for making decisions. Whenever I made an improper decision, I always said that I had turned it over to my Higher Power. I blamed the mistake on Him. Of course, the reality was I had made the mistake myself.

Then one day I admitted to making a choice, and things went a lot easier. What I discovered was that I could ask my Higher Power for help, but then I had to make choices. It's funny how the Third Step works for me. I'm just glad it works.

✍

I started in Alateen about four years ago because my mother's drinking was overwhelming my life. I was concentrating on her drinking so much that I put everything else in my life on hold. As a result, things were really building up inside of me.

Then one of my friends told me about Alateen. Because I needed something, desperately, I went.

I've never regretted going to Alateen. I've found the kind of people who let me talk openly about what's going on in my life. They understand my problems, because they've had them too. With their help, I've gotten things back together in my life.

Today, my mother is still drinking. But the difference for me is that today I can live my life without having to live my mother's life. I've given my mother's life to my Higher Power. Because of Alateen, I can detach from my mother, and still love her a lot.

✍

After I had my sight damaged during one of my mother's rages, I resented her. I blamed her for everything that was happening to me because she hit me so hard.

I thought I would never be able to live a normal life because of my handicap. I thought I'd probably always be dependent on someone else, even to go shopping near my house. Because I was so resentful, I moved away from God. Things got worse at home, in school, with my teachers, and with my friends and relatives.

I went through this experience for two years, telling myself that I didn't need God or anyone else. I didn't do my school work. I didn't do much of anything—except I started hating myself. It was at this time that I came into Alateen.

In Alateen I started realizing how wrong I was. Listening to the members share their personal stories, I regained my faith in God and in people. I understood that I wasn't the only one who suffered because of alcoholism. Many kids were going through worse problems than I was. Slowly, I began accepting my problems and myself.

Today I trust God, completely. I'm grateful to be in Alateen. I'm grateful to receive all the support and understanding from my friends in the group. Thank you, everyone.

✍

My most disturbing experience was when my dad was in a horrible accident. His truck was hit by a train.

I thought all hope was lost. I prayed to my Higher Power and asked Him to help my dad, but nothing happened.

It took so long that I finally gave up. As soon as I gave up, my dad started to respond.

Today my dad is okay, and soon he'll be able to live on his own again. I'll just turn things over to my Higher Power, and I'll keep on praying.

✍

Alateen has helped me through a lot of things. My dad left. My mom got remarried. A close friend committed suicide.

I've decided that none of them happened because of me, and I can't change any of them. But I can still have a happy life.

Letting go and letting God is what the Third Step is all about to me. My sponsor told me I can grieve and feel real sad, but I need to let go. She was right.

With my Alateen program and my friends and my Higher Power, I can be as happy as I want, any time I want.

✍

When I started in the
Alateen program, I
thought that God didn't
love me or even like me.
When I saw that others
were convinced that God
loved them, even though they made mistakes, it made me want to give God a try.

I started by giving Him my little
things, and they worked out all right
without me having to do anything. So I
gave Him more things, and those worked
out too. The more I believed He loved me,
the happier I became.

So the relationship kept growing, 'til
now I can see Him working major miracles
in my life and in other people's lives.

In Alateen I learned to separate people from the things they do. My father is the alcoholic in my family. When I was twelve years old he molested me.

That was four years ago when I first started Alateen. When I came to Alateen I hated my father. I never wanted to see him again. But Alateen taught me to separate him from his actions.

I realize now that I love my father, but I hate what he did to me. Eventually, I'll outgrow the pain he caused me, but it won't be easy. As long as I have Alateen I'll have the support and guidance to get through it.

I have turned my life and my will over to the care of a power that's greater than I am. I know I'm in good hands.

✍

I came into the program desperate and confused. I was angry and scared, and I felt like everybody was better than I was. But in Alateen I discovered that I wasn't the only one living in pain.

I stopped feeling inadequate because I learned that the people who are really serene have their Higher Power to thank for it. I also discovered that a lot of the kids at my school who looked so perfect were really dying inside.

My Higher Power became my comfort. Through Him I can get that peace of mind that I've always wanted. It doesn't mean that I have to have some big, secret knowledge. All I have to have is the belief that there is love out there.

My Higher Power gave me Alateen to help me understand that I don't have to do it all by myself. I just tell myself that God doesn't take something away without putting something better in its place.

✍

God wasn't a big part of my life until recently. When my dad went into recovery, everything went downhill.

I thought God wasn't going to take care of us, so I depended on myself. When I started to get into even worse shape, I asked God to take care of me.

Now I know that He will take care of me, because little miracles have already started to happen in my life. I've begun to trust God, and I've begun to accept what He has done for me and my family.

My life is unmanageable when I try to control other people. When I find myself getting a controlling attitude, I look to my Higher Power. I ask Him to take care of the situation any way He wishes.

Once I'm out of His way, He does what's best for me. It may not be what I had thought was best, but in the long run things work out better than if I'd tried to impose my will on the situation.

My Higher Power knows an infinite amount more than I do. I've decided to step aside and let Him help me.

Workshop On
STEP THREE

Made a decision to turn our will and our lives over to the care of God as we understood Him.

Complete the following sentences, adding as many sentences as you want.

When I decide to turn over my will and my life, I ...

When I picture the God of my understanding, I see ...

I turn my will and my life over to the care of my Higher Power by ...

STEP FOUR

Made a searching and fearless moral inventory of ourselves.

In the first two Steps we admitted the truth about what happened in our lives and we began to believe that God, or something more powerful than we are, could help us think clearly and calmly again. In Step Three we made a decision to let our Higher Power help us, so we would not have to feel so afraid.

It is a good idea to work the Steps in order, because each Step helps make it easier for us to work the next one. Without working the first three Steps, Step Four is too difficult for most of us. We might shy away from looking at the truth about ourselves; we might feel fearful instead of feeling fearless.

So, what is a searching and fearless moral inventory of ourselves? It is a thorough and honest way to describe who we are. It can be a list of descriptions about ourselves, or it can be our own personal story. Because our Higher Power is helping us, we can look at the truth about ourselves without feeling terrified. If we still feel a lot of fear, we can go back and do Step Three again to get more help and reassurance before we continue with Step Four.

Some of us may think that we already know the truth

about ourselves. It is still worthwhile to do the Fourth Step because we might discover that we have been taking someone else's word for who we are. The real truth might be that we are far more valuable and lovable than other people have led us to believe. Step Four can help us appreciate who we are. Even if we have made big mistakes we are still valuable and lovable people. *Alateen's Fourth Step Inventory* workbook can be a handy guide for working Step Four. Al-Anon's *Blueprint For Progress* can also help.

Alateens share on
STEP FOUR

Some of my good qualities are: I'm smart, I'm a good listener, I'm understanding, independent, responsible and funny. I'm also likable, caring, supportive, sensitive, trustworthy, and reliable.

When someone criticizes me, first I start to wonder why they're picking on me. Then I usually stop, listen, and learn.

It was hard to accept myself, though, at first. I thought I was the worst person I knew and that no one would like me for myself. Then I went away on an Alateen weekend event and did my Fourth Step inventory. I got to know myself and, at first, I didn't like myself very much. The whole idea of the Fourth Step and self-acceptance was so new to me. But gradually I began to learn about myself, and the most amazing thing happened—I started to love me.

I decided I don't have to try to be something I'm not. I've learned that I can accept myself, bad and good. Sometimes I still have doubts, but that's okay. I don't have to be perfect.

✍

I used to feel like people were constantly judging me. But I was a people-pleaser, too. I wanted people to like me and accept me, so I changed my appearance and my values so I could be part of the crowd.

Today, I realize that I was making a big deal out of something that wasn't very big. Sure, some people still judge me. But my Alateen friends don't. My Alateen friends don't care what kind of clothes I wear, what kind of music I listen to, or how many sports I play. My Alateen friends love me and accept me because I'm making the effort to get help. They show me that no matter what I do, they'll always love me. Today, I can dress the way I want to dress. I can have my own opinions, and I can feel free to be myself—no questions asked.

✍

Alateen has done a lot for me. The most help I've gotten came from doing the Fourth and Fifth Steps. The kids in my group didn't care about the mistakes I'd made. They only wanted to help me learn that alcoholism is a disease.

All of us have been affected by alcoholism somehow. It's just that we've reacted to it in different ways. We need to recognize our own reactions. Then we can decide whether we want to continue reacting in the same old ways, or if maybe we want to try something new.

I'm learning how to study myself. I'm figuring out what makes me tick, without putting myself down.

✍

I used to be very depressed and very shy. I hardly said anything to anybody. I felt like I was worthless and that nobody cared about me.

After taking my Fourth Step inventory I'm beginning to realize that I have a lot of abilities. I'm even starting to feel a little bit special. It's a brand new feeling for me. I'm even learning how to be more outgoing.

It helps when I go ahead and talk in my Alateen meetings. I have a lot of new friends, thanks to the program. And one of my new friends is me. I just needed to get to know myself a little better.

Sometimes with friends I found myself compromising my time and doing what they wanted me to do, rather than focusing on my own needs. I didn't feel like I was very smart or very creative.

In Alateen I've learned that I am my own person, just like everyone else is their own person. I look at myself with more confidence now. I can't cause, control, or cure anybody of anything, but I can make my own decisions.

I've always had a problem with dating. I thought the way to get a date was to be one of the coolest people around. I thought I had to be popular, dress nicely in expensive clothes, and have money.

But that way didn't work for me. The way I tried to achieve it was to ditch my old friends because they weren't popular. I also tried to buy new friends. It cost me a lot of money and a lot of heartache.

I never had a date before I came to Alateen because I didn't have anything real to offer anybody. I was a fake. When I started working the Twelve Steps, I came across a step that said, "Made a searching and fearless moral inventory of ourselves."

When I took this inventory I found the real me, and I found that I had a lot to offer other people. This Step showed me what it meant to be a friend. I think that's why I have dates now, because I'm myself and nobody else.

✍

Before Alateen, whenever I made mistakes I'd get really mad at myself. I tried to ignore my mistakes, and I tried to be perfect. But now, I know I'm not perfect. Now in Alateen I don't ignore my mistakes anymore. I've actually learned how to use them.

Every time I make a mistake I try to learn something from it. Most of the time it really helps. I'm really thankful for Alateen.

✍

When my life got hard I used to take a drink. Because my mom drank, and I thought she did it just to hurt me, I decided to pay her back.

But now I know I need to take responsibility for myself, no matter what anybody else does. I can't drink or do something else to hurt myself just to get back at other people.

I try to keep this in mind whenever someone upsets or hurts me.

✍

When I was a little girl I had very low self-esteem. I had no real father, only a step-father who used to drink and do drugs.

My big problem was that I was fat. I had a hard time in school and at home. Because I was fat, everyone said that I was a nobody. People called me terrible names.

When I was in junior high school my best friend started going to Alateen. I went to a few meetings because she asked me to go. It took me about a year before I started to work any kind of a program. In the meantime I tried to get attention any way that I could. I know now that I tried to get the wrong kind of attention. I ended up getting raped.

I know now that it wasn't my fault, but at the time I thought it was all my fault. I was being told that I was nothing but a scared, fat, stupid slut. Actually, guys were just taking advantage of my low self-esteem. I finally started working my program. The Alateens and my Alateen sponsor helped me realize that I'm not a bad person. They pointed out that a lot of people really love me and care about me.

Now I use my Twelve Steps, the Slogans, and the Serenity Prayer. I'm getting a lot of help with my self-esteem and with my future.

✍

I've always had a problem facing reality, because I've always made a dream world for myself. I'll dream about being skinnier, prettier, more popular — just about anything else that I think I would like to be, except myself.

My habit of living in a dream world really hurts me. You know what happens? When I finally snap out of my dream, then reality hits me right in the face, and I become depressed.

In Alateen I have people tell me that I'm great just the way I am. I love hearing that. Now I know they're going to say it even before they open their mouths. It's very supportive when they do that for me.

At first I couldn't believe that this support was real. Do you know what I mean? I thought maybe I was still dreaming, but every time I come back to the meeting those Alateens are still there, still telling me that I'm okay. All I have to do is look at the truth about myself and work on my Fourth Step inventory.

✐

I had a lot of guilt. I thought I was a bad person and God was punishing me.

I tried to be perfect. I kept my room clean, got good grades in school, and I never got into trouble. I felt responsible for so many things that when something bad happened I couldn't let people know that it was my fault. I thought everything was my fault.

Alateen helped me accept that I was not responsible for everything that happened. Letting go of all that guilt and responsibility was a great relief. Now it's easier for me to admit I am wrong when something really is my fault.

Now I know deep down inside that I'm a decent person. I can even love myself. I'm really glad I don't have to be perfect anymore.

Something important that I've learned about myself is a habit I have of trying to please everyone. I guess I've always tried to figure out what people wanted me to be. Then I'd do my best to be what they wanted.

The trouble is I always ended up being a different person, depending on who was with me. When it was my alcoholic father who was with me, whether he was sober or not, I felt like I was supposed to be small. If I made myself small, then I was making my father bigger than he really was.

I didn't realize what I was doing, but I was giving my father more power over me. Because I never knew what he was going to say or do, I felt scared all the time. Even after he'd been sober for a long time, I still felt the same way.

After I learned these things about myself in my Fourth Step, I found out that it wasn't my responsibility to make my dad feel big. It wasn't my fault if my dad drank or not. It wasn't my fault whatever he decided to do or not do. He is the master of his own thoughts, feelings and actions. And I am the master of mine.

This was amazing to me. I know I'd probably heard it a hundred times before — of course it wasn't my fault what other people did. But I never connected it with my habit of pleasing other people all the time.

Every day I'm learning something new to help me cope with my family and myself. I don't feel like an "old-timer," even though I've been in Alateen for over two years now, because I'm still powerless over alcohol. But today my mind doesn't have to spin trying to make everyone else feel happy all the time. I'm learning how to relax and be myself, no matter who is with me, thanks to Alateen and especially to my sponsor and my friends who helped me try the Fourth Step.

The most painful experience of my life was when my father told me that I wasn't good enough to be his daughter. I felt completely devastated. Fortunately for me, I was in Alateen at the time.

At my very next meeting I told my group what had happened and what my father had said. My group helped me by introducing me to the Fourth Step. They suggested that I set aside some time to get to know about myself, including a lot of the good things that I know about the kind of person I am. I was encouraged to write these things down and to keep my writing in a safe place. It was important for me to know where the safe hiding place would be before I started writing. After a while it really didn't matter what anyone else thought about me, including my dad. What mattered was what I thought about myself.

I'm very grateful to my Alateen group for helping me learn how to appreciate myself. You know, the whole world looks different to me now.

The Fourth Step in Alateen helped me accept that I used to be pretty irresponsible. I used to do a lot of things right away, without thinking first about what I was going to do. It caused a lot of anger and heartache for myself and others.

I've learned a lot about myself. As a result, my self-esteem is higher than ever. I've learned that I make mistakes, but I've learned that I'm not a mistake.

Now I have a great job. I work well with other people. I'm considered a very responsible person — all because I learned to take a minute to think about what I'm going to do, before I do it.

I always wondered how people could learn from their own mistakes. Now I know.

✍

I'm very fortunate that I've had Alateen for the past two years, and that I've learned how to love. Before Alateen I considered suicide, faced other people's deaths, faced hell for real in the occult, and the challenges go on and on.

I could have given up, but I haven't. I've always turned the right way in a crisis. I've surrendered, accepted, and seen who my true friends are — the friends I've made through Alateen.

I've learned to accept and love myself. I'm not super girl, and I'm not asking for applause. I am me, and I'm okay. I may not be physically beautiful, but that's not half as important as being internally beautiful — and I am a beautiful person. Because I've come to realize that, I can love now, and I can be loved.

I still have a long way to go before I'm even close to being perfect. That's okay, too. I just want to stay my own best friend. I want to give my life a real good chance.

✍

I first started in an Alateen group for younger members a long time ago. I started coming with my grandmother who was the alcoholic in my family. She's been sober now for almost fifteen years.

I really don't remember what it was like when I started Alateen, but I do remember the last four years. I remember coming into Alateen every Wednesday and thinking I was at a carnival, playing games and being disruptive. I started to realize that I needed to change because people were beginning to dislike me.

I needed to change for myself because I wasn't getting anything out of the way I was acting. I was building a wall of anger inside of myself while I was trying to change everybody else. So I started coming with a zipper over my mouth. I just listened.

I began to hear that others were having the same kind of problems that I was having. And then I started to share my feelings. I found that it really worked. Coming to meetings with my ears open and my mouth shut helped me get good suggestions to try in my life. Sharing my problems instead of causing problems helped keep my anger from building up inside of me. Today, Alateen is a great part of my life.

Workshop On
STEP FOUR

Made a searching and fearless moral inventory of ourselves.

Complete the following sentences, adding as many sentences as you want.

For me, making a moral inventory is like ...

When I look at the good things about myself, I see ...

When I look at the things I don't like about myself, I ...

I take a moral inventory of myself by ...

STEP FIVE

Admitted to God, to ourselves and to another human being the exact nature of our wrongs.

Although God knows the truth about us already, when we share our truth with God or our Higher Power we develop a stronger spiritual connection and a more loving relationship. When we admit the truth about us to ourselves we give ourselves permission to love the person we really are. When we admit the truth about ourselves to another human being, we give permission for other people to love us, too.

When is a good time for us to do Step Five? When we have finished the Fourth Step and we want to grow some more we can look for a special person we trust to help us with Step Five. It is usually best to ask someone in Alateen or Al-Anon, especially someone who has already done their own Fourth and Fifth Step. It is also possible to ask a spiritual leader or a guidance counselor.

The focus for what we share about ourselves in Step Five is the exact nature of our wrongs. What can that be? It can be the habits we have formed, the things that we tend to do without thinking very much. It can be the way we react to people and things around us. It can be the ways that we learned to protect ourselves when we felt threatened. It can be things that we have done, or it can be things that we have failed to do.

The purpose of Step Five is to help us accept the truth about the ways that we have acted. The purpose isn't to judge, criticize or scold ourselves; nor is it to flatter, brag or gloat about ourselves. The purpose is to get to know who we really are by studying our own actions. This includes identifying the things that we really like about ourselves, as well as the things that we don't like.

For many of us Steps Four and Five mark the real beginning of our recovery from the impact of someone else's alcoholism. If we can get really honest about ourselves in these Steps, then we can give ourselves a fresh start at life. If not, then maybe we can make at least a little bit of progress in that direction. If Steps Four and Five are just too hard right now, maybe spending more time on Step Three will give us what we need to make the process a little easier.

Alateens share on
STEP FIVE

My sponsor listened to my horror stories about myself, and when we were done she stood up, held out her arms, and she hugged me.

If she could know the real me and still love me, then I thought maybe I was still worth something. If my parents had heard the same exact things, I think they would have killed me.

For the first time, I found out that by being honest about myself with someone, I could still be loved. I think that experience has changed my life, forever.

✍

I used to keep things bottled up inside of me, thinking that no one wanted to hear about my problems. When I came to Alateen I learned that it's better to get things out in the open. It's not good to keep things locked up inside of me to rattle my brain.

A lot of the energy I've used, thinking about the problems I have, could have been used to make me happy.

Sharing with others in the program, who have gone through the same things I have, eases my mind. I'm a happier person today because I'm not still carrying around yesterday's garbage.

✍

Growing up, I never had anyone I could totally confide in. I always felt I had to hide part of myself. I also felt that if someone knew the real me I wouldn't have any friends. I always felt afraid of what people might think of me.

I didn't have a major turn around when I came to Alateen. The change was gradual. The person who helped me the most in my change was my Alateen sponsor. I could relate to her so well. She made me realize things about myself that I didn't quite understand. Without her help, I wouldn't be where I am now.

My sponsor helped me to accept change. I was always afraid to do anything new. Without her help I wouldn't have led my first meeting, which really helped me in my growing process. I wouldn't have started working the Steps. I wouldn't have told anybody my secrets, and I'd still be trapped in yesterday.

✍

All the adults I knew had the idea that my life was perfect — you know, nothing but fun and games. Of course, they got this idea mainly from me. I always looked so happy-go-lucky on the outside. On the inside there was a whole different picture of the real me.

But I didn't know how to let people know what my life was really like. One problem was carrying my 59-year-old father upstairs to put him to bed. Another was how to smile when I don't know if I'll find my dad dead someday when I get home from school. Or how I can explain to my friends that they can't come over to my house because my dad is drunk.

In Alateen I can be honest, both with kids and with adults. It's a big relief. I don't know what I would do if I couldn't be honest about my life with somebody.

Right now I'm having problems at school. I got a deficiency notice saying that I'm going to get a failing grade in math. All of my other classes are going very well. In fact, my achievement scores show that I'm way ahead of my age group.

It's hard for me to admit that I'm failing in math. I feel like there's something wrong with me. So I struggle with myself. I try to pretend like there's nothing wrong. Then, finally, I admit that I'm failing in math.

Guess what? When I admitted what was happening, then I felt better. When I started feeling better, then I was able to do something to improve my math grade.

✍

When I was young I needed to be an adult to survive in an alcoholic home, so I tried being really mature to gain the respect and love from my parents.

Alateen taught me that the most important person to gain respect and love from is myself.

Now that I'm an adult, I can be a kid and mature at the same time, because maturity means something else to me now. First, it means being able to cope with the responsibilities I have in a serene way. Second, it means to be as honest as possible with myself and others.

Humility frees me from outside pressures and allows me to learn at any time from anyone or any experience. Being able to admit and correct my faults has given me self-respect and self-love. It also gives me many true friends who love and respect me as much as I love and respect them.

Even my parents love and respect me now!

Workshop On
STEP FIVE

Admitted to God, to ourselves and to another human being the exact nature of our wrongs.

Complete the following sentences, adding as many sentences as you want.

I admit to <u>God</u> what I really learned about myself in the Fourth Step by...

When I admit to <u>myself</u> what I have learned about myself in the Fourth Step, I...

When I admit to <u>someone</u> else what I have learned about myself in the Fourth Step, I ...

STEP SIX

Were entirely ready to have God remove all these defects of character.

Our honesty and openness in working the first five Steps have prepared us to do Step Six. The key to Step Six is that God removes our defects of character. It is our job to become entirely ready for this to happen. If we have trouble knowing what our defects are, we can always back up and spend a little more time on Step Five or Step Four.

For many of us our defects of character come out when we feel stressed or afraid. So how do we relax and feel safe? We can take such good care of ourselves that we do not feel tempted to use our old ways. We can watch for the need to HALT and give ourselves special attention when we are feeling **H**ungry or **A**ngry or **L**onely or **T**ired. We can have fun. We can talk about our feelings with our Alateen and Al-Anon friends.

When we are taking good care of ourselves we usually don't need our defects of character to protect us. When we don't need them, it is easy to feel ready to have our Higher Power remove them.

I hurt myself the most when I'm extremely mad. While I'm spending all of my time and energy hating someone, I could be doing a lot of other things, like doing my homework or having fun.

If I'm so mad that I can't even concentrate, then my life suffers. So now when I get mad I try to do something else until I cool down. I like to listen to music or go to an Alateen meeting. If I can talk in a meeting about why I feel so mad, then I leave feeling normal again.

✍

Before I came to Alateen I would pile on the make-up. I needed to look good. I'd carry myself as though I had no self-respect. It was crazy. I was trying to call attention to myself at the same time that I was trying to hide. I wanted people to notice me but I didn't want to have any contact with anyone.

So I threw myself into school or anything else to get my mind off the fact that no one liked me—how could they? I didn't let anyone get to know who I was. But most important of all, I didn't like myself.

Listening to people my own age share about the Steps helped me to quit obsessing about my looks. Gradually, I even learned to express myself at meetings. Listening is what did it for me. It helped me get ready to let the real me come out.

Not everyone likes being around me today, but a lot of people do. And guess what? I like myself.

When I came to Alateen I thought I knew everything there was to know. I also judged people by how much money they had or what kind of clothes they wore. But Alateen showed me the real meaning of friendship and knowledge.

I've been in the program for eight years now, and I've learned a lot. Not everything, but a lot. I no longer judge people by their money or their clothes. To find out the truth about a person, I have to look deeper than his or her appearance.

I once told one of my Alateen friends, "You're lucky I found the fellowship, or I wouldn't have ever talked to you!" She just laughed and said, "I know, but I love you anyway."

That's the kind of friend you'll find in Alateen. And that's the kind of love you'll get.

Workshop On
STEP SIX

Were entirely ready to have God remove all these defects of character.

Complete the following sentences, adding as many sentences as you want.

To me, defects of character means ...

I become ready to have God take away all my defects by...

Some of the things I can do to take care of myself are ...

Some of my defects of character are ...

STEP SEVEN

Humbly asked Him to remove our shortcomings.

Thanks to Step Six, we became ready to have our Higher Power remove all of our defects of character. So what is the difference between our defects of character and our shortcomings? To many people, defects and shortcomings are the same exact thing. To others, shortcomings have to do with effort.

If we believe that defects and shortcomings are the same thing, then all we have to deal with is the part about being humble when we ask our Higher Power to remove them. Since humility, or being humble, has to do with honesty, Steps Four, Five and Six have given us lots of practice already. Honestly asked Him to remove our shortcomings is a good way to read this Step.

What if shortcomings are not the same exact thing as defects of character? What if shortcomings have to do with our efforts? Maybe when we ask our Higher Power to remove our shortcomings we are asking Him to remove those parts of our lives where we are falling short. Maybe our big problem is not so much what we are doing wrong. Maybe we are simply not doing enough of the things that we know are the right things to do. Maybe we don't know how.

How do we know which way is the right way for us? We know because of what we learned about ourselves in our Fourth and Fifth Steps. All of us can try to do more of the things that we do right and fewer of the things that we do wrong. Deep down inside, we know which is which. Maybe that is what the word humbly refers to; it is not just the truth, it is the truth that we know deep down inside of us.

Alateens Share On
STEP SEVEN

My dad is the alcoholic in my family. He started drinking long before I was born. Even though his problem was older than I am, I took on the responsibility for it. And I couldn't handle it.

I worried about my dad so much that I made myself sick. I got so depressed that I was close to suicide. I was put into a hospital where the doctors told me that I had to stop worrying about my dad. They told me I needed to concentrate on taking care of myself. When they let me out of the hospital, they told me to go to Alateen.

In Alateen it took me over a year to get to the Seventh Step. The Seventh Step was the easiest step I've ever taken in the program. It took me just a few minutes to ask God to please help me stop worrying so much about my dad.

Now it's not just my dad that I love a lot. I also love everybody in Alateen. But I don't have to worry about anyone.

Ever since my mom and dad divorced I've felt like it's my responsibility to take care of my mother and my little sister. I've turned into pretty much of a people-pleaser.

For some reason, it seems like I need to have everybody like me. The way I do it is to put on little shows for everyone. I change my feelings and my ideas about things, depending on who I'm with. I've been doing this for so long I've forgotten who I am. I feel like I'm just one big zero. I feel like I don't count for anything. I'm just something that everyone else throws away.

My mom always tells me that I am a very depressed and withdrawn person. I know it's true. I'm trying to get to know myself better. I would very much like to have my Higher Power remove all of these things that are wrong with me. I don't want to be a nobody anymore.

Until I came to Alateen, I had no idea that naps could be good for me. Now when I think about getting myself ready for something important, I think about whether or not I've had enough sleep. I never even thought about that before. It didn't matter to me whether I felt good or not.

Now, if I'm getting myself ready for something that's really important, I try to plan ahead to take at least a half hour or forty-five minute nap. I know it sounds weird, but I think my Higher Power takes away a lot of my character defects when I get enough sleep. I'm glad Alateen taught me some of the little things that I can do to take better care of myself.

Whenever I feel angry I just take a deep breath, and I ask God to take my anger away. Then I usually feel a lot better.

When I first came to Alateen I was a mess. I figured if my mother didn't have to take care of herself, then neither did I. My clothes were crumpled and my hair was messy and I was filthy. My school work was awful, so I was failing sixth grade—I didn't even care.

Two years later, my grades are up. I wear nice clothes, and my hair is neat and clean.

All of this change didn't come easily, and it didn't happen overnight. It came from time in my Alateen meetings and wanting to change. And it came from asking my Higher Power to help me.

At my first Alateen meeting I was scared of sharing my thoughts and troubles. But I took it one day at a time. I've found that Alateen has young people with almost the same problems that I've always had.

Today I know that the alcoholic's drinking is not my problem. It's the alcoholic's problem. The only place I could have learned that was in Alateen. I know that if I'm angry at the alcoholic in my life I can call my sponsor or Alateens my age. I can share my problems with them.

And I can ask my Higher Power to take away some of my old ways of reacting. I'm glad I came to Alateen, because if I didn't I would still feel very alone and very scared.

Workshop On
STEP SEVEN

Humbly asked Him to remove our shortcomings.

Complete the following sentences, adding as many sentences as you want.

To me, being humble is ...

When I humbly and honestly ask God to remove my shortcomings, I ...

Some of my shortcomings are...

I know I'm entirely ready to have shortcomings removed when ...

When I think of my shortcomings, I ...

Am I asking or am I telling? What is the difference?

STEP EIGHT

Made a list of all persons we had harmed, and became willing to make amends to them all.

The first part of Step Eight is the easy part. All we have to do is make a list. Some of us know the names of all the people we have harmed, because they are usually the same people who mean the most to us. If we have trouble figuring out whom we have harmed, another approach is to make a list of all the people with whom we wish we had a better relationship. We can talk about it to another member or our sponsor. We may want to include ourselves on our list.

The second part of Step Eight might be more difficult. It asks us to become willing to make amends to all of those people. Making amends is kind of like making up with someone after you've had a disagreement or a fight. It can mean telling someone that you are sorry about something. It can also mean changing the way that you treat this person. It may mean doing whatever you can to mend your relationship.

But how can you become willing to make amends to someone you don't like? How can you make amends to someone you are still angry at? One way is to divide the list into three parts. The first part can be a list of the people that you are very willing to make amends to. The second part can be a list of all those that <u>maybe</u> you are willing to make amends to. The third list is those you feel you definitely will <u>never</u> be willing to make amends to.

Keep these lists in a safe place. If and when you ever change your mind about making amends to someone, take the name off the old list and put it on another. By recognizing the possibility of changing your mind, you are showing your willingness to make amends to everyone.

Alateens Share On
STEP EIGHT

One night at my Alateen meeting our sponsor gave all of us a piece of paper. She said to make a list of all the people that we'd like to have a better relationship with.

The more I sat there and stared at my paper, the more upset I felt. There are a lot of people that I'd like to have a better relationship with, starting with my mom. I could feel myself starting to cry. Finally, one of my friends said, "What are we going to do with these names?" Our sponsor said, "We aren't going to do anything with the names—the list is just for you to have for yourself. You can keep it, or you can throw it away."

Suddenly, everybody started writing.

✍

The list of people I have harmed is pretty long. My little brothers are on the top of the list. I did some pretty mean things to them, especially when I used to baby-sit. The rest of the list are all my friends, and of course my folks.

The main way that I harmed the people I really care about is by not being myself. Until I came to Alateen I really didn't know or like myself very much. My dad didn't seem to approve of me, so I learned very early how to hide myself and my feelings. Since it wasn't a good idea for me to be myself around my dad, I guess I just started hiding myself from everyone. I didn't know what else to do until I started getting help in Alateen.

I'm still afraid to be myself, completely. I guess I need to put myself on the list of the people I've harmed. Maybe I've even harmed myself the most.

✍

For a long time, I knew exactly where my Eighth Step list was. It was on the corner of my desk at home. Once in a while I even picked it up. I'd give myself a hard time about not doing anything with it—you know, like using it for a Ninth Step.

When I told my sponsor about what I was doing to myself, he said, "Remember to give yourself credit for making the list." He also said I could start talking about becoming willing to make amends to the names on the list. He said in the Eighth Step I didn't have to make amends—I just had to become willing to make amends.

✍

One of the ways I made my list of people I'd harmed was to look at my Fourth and Fifth Steps. Some of the things I'd written about my life in my Fourth Step made me think of certain people's names right away. In fact, when I was thinking about them I could see their faces in my mind. Seeing their faces helped me to feel willing to make amends to them. It was hard sometimes, but I'm glad I did it.

✍

I taped a list of names on my mirror, so when I got up in the morning I could add any names that I felt like adding. It was easier for me to just write the names early in the day, so I didn't have a whole long time to think about it.

The other thing that I did with my list was to read it every night before I went to bed.

✍

When my dad was drinking I didn't have anyone telling me what to do, or when and how to do it. I was making my own decisions. Mainly, it was like I didn't have a father.

Then my dad went in for recovery. It was like some guy just popped into my life and started trying to be my dad. All of a sudden, someone was right there making all of my decisions for me. I felt like I wanted to get into trouble.

It was really hard for me to accept someone telling me what to do. I was used to doing what I wanted. I even wished my dad would start drinking again, just so I could do what I wanted to do. But since then I've gotten to know my dad a little better. Plus, I've gotten to hear what other people my age are going through, thanks to my Alateen group. I know now that my dad is just trying to get me on the right track, so I won't end up like he did.

I'm going to apologize to him pretty soon. It was just hard for me to adjust to his new way of doing things. It still is.

Workshop On
STEP EIGHT

Made a list of all persons we had harmed, and became willing to make amends to them all.

Complete the following sentences, adding as many sentences as you want.

I can start to make a list of persons I have harmed by ...

When I make a list of all the people I've treated badly, I ...

Being willing to make amends means ...

I can become willing to make amends by ...

When I have become willing to make amends, I ...

STEP NINE

Made direct amends to such people wherever possible, except when to do so would injure them or others.

Something wonderful happens when we sincerely say, "I'm sorry." We forgive ourselves. Sometimes the person to whom we offer the amends will also forgive us. That can be a very special moment for both people. Our success with Step Nine, however, does not depend on what the other person does.

Before we offer amends to someone it is very important to consider their feelings. If we believe our offer will make them or someone else feel bad, then we need to stop. It is not okay for us to hurt someone. Maybe we can make our amends to them in another way, such as by treating them better than we have treated them in the past. Maybe we cannot go near the person at all. In that case we might have to find some other way of dealing with Step Nine. Maybe we can make a donation to charity, or visit people at a nursing home or in a children's hospital. We might pray for the person or do an anonymous good deed for someone else.

Step Nine can always be a wonderful experience for us.

The people I really needed to make amends to were my grandparents. Unfortunately, they had already died before I knew what Step Nine was all about.

The way that I discovered I could still make amends to them was to get involved with service work. I know they would be proud to see me representing my group at assemblies and conferences. They always wanted the best for me, and I usually managed to let them down. Now I like to think that maybe they can see me take my first turn at being secretary or leading beginner meetings.

A lot of things I'm getting from Alateen are the same things that my grandparents tried to give me. I was too caught up in my own little world to appreciate what they were trying to give me when they were alive. It feels good today to begin to get closer to becoming the kind of granddaughter that I believe they always wanted me to be.

I know my Higher Power is taking good care of them. I get a certain satisfaction out of thinking that my Higher Power is letting them know that I'm taking good care of myself.

The hardest Step for me to do is making amends. I've made them to most of the people I've hurt, but there are still some names on my list. Before Alateen, my life was worthless, and I couldn't wait for it to end. Now my life is pretty good, and I enjoy every minute of it. Working the Steps has given me my life back. I'm willing to do the tough stuff now, because it works. It really works.

I've always been the one who would do anything for anybody, just to get them to like me. Lately, I've been making amends to myself.

I've been learning to set limits with my grandma. She always expected me to take her to stores and other places. Then I would stop all my plans so I could please her.

Now I've learned to still be there for her, but on my time too. I set a time aside when I can help her, but I take time for my needs too. That way, I can help her and still be helping myself.

Thanks, Alateen!

My father died unexpectedly. He was a recovering alcoholic in the program of Alcoholics Anonymous. His death was the most terrible thing that ever happened to me.

It was terrible because I had never faced up to the fact that my dad was an alcoholic. I hadn't faced up to the fact that his drinking affected my life. Somehow at fifteen years old I was too wrapped up in myself to even think I cared. But I did care. After he died I found myself wanting to ask him a lot of questions.

I wanted to know why he drank and how he quit drinking. I wanted to know how he could have so much faith in God. I really regret not being in Alateen when my dad died. I felt completely lost.

One day, about a year and a half after my father died, a good friend of mine asked me to go to Alateen with her. I was so afraid that I would be rejected because the alcoholic in my family was dead. I wasn't sure I wanted to go, but I knew I had to do something. I was tired of living in denial of the truth about my dad and my life.

No one rejected me at that first Alateen meeting I attended. In fact, I found myself accepted. Everyone there listened to me.

I still have a lot of guilt about how I never talked straight to my father about his alcoholism. I still grieve for him and what I lost, even now, three years later. Alateen has helped me realize that my dad's alcoholism wasn't my fault. I've also been able to forgive him and myself, slowly. I'm still angry and hurt deep inside, but Alateen has helped me to grow and even to heal a few wounds. If I didn't have the Alateen group with all its openness and understanding, I would still be where I was three years ago when my father died. Now I understand the Serenity Prayer that my dad had hanging on his bedroom wall, and I'm learning to appreciate my life, one day at a time.

✍🏻

For a long time I felt numb. Nothing mattered. No one mattered. I just barely got from one day to the next. I reminded myself of the way my mom used to be.

When my mother wasn't drinking, she was taking sedatives and tranquilizers. Most of the time she acted like nothing meant anything. She acted like I didn't matter. Somehow I got the message that I was the main problem in her life. If it wasn't for me, then my mom would be happy.

I got that message from my mom, but when I came to Alateen I learned that my mom was wrong. I learned that I am a good person, and I learned that people can love me.

For awhile I hated my mother for making me feel worthless. My sponsor suggested that I write a letter to myself. He suggested that I write myself the kind of letter my mother would write to me if she was a healthy and happy lady. You know, all of the neat things in that letter were true. I know my mom would have said those things to me if she could.

Now I can't see my mother anymore, and she never recovered from her disease. But I know she finally knows that I love her.

A couple of weeks ago I was just about ready to give up. I was so depressed about my cancer. Even though I was getting better, I felt scared. I was scared that people who didn't know what was wrong with me would laugh.

I had the chance to go to a couple of Al-Anon/Alateen conferences, but for some reason I felt so out of place. I realize now why I felt that way. I wasn't very happy with myself.

I had to begin again. I was right back at the beginning, but at least I was starting to admit just how powerless I was feeling and how unmanageable my life was. And pretty soon I could feel my own face breaking into a smile.

I think I was making amends to myself.

Workshop On
STEP NINE

Made direct amends to such people wherever possible, except when to do so would injure them or others.

Complete the following sentences, adding as many sentences as you want.

To me making amends means that I ...

When I tell people through my <u>words</u> that I'd like to treat them better than I used to treat them, I ...

When I tell people through my <u>actions</u> that I'd like to treat them better than I used to treat them, I ...

Some ways I can make amends to others without harming them are ...

Making amends is important to me because ...

If I try to make amends to someone and they don't accept it, then I ...

I know when I am making amends to someone because...

STEP TEN

Continued to take personal inventory and when we were wrong promptly admitted it.

Step Ten continues the same process that we used for Step Four. The difference is we try to do Step Ten more frequently, such as every night before we go to sleep. When we review the actions we took during the day it is important to look at what we like as well as what we do not like.

We deserve all of the encouragement we can get to do more of the things that we like. Acknowledging what we like about our actions will give us permission to do more. Admitting our mistakes helps us to forgive ourselves. Eventually we will get to the point where we can recognize our mistakes right away, even before we have finished making them. If we work to change our behavior, we won't have to make amends continually to the same people for the same behavior.

Through Step Ten we are giving ourselves fresh opportunities to do our best every day. We are keeping our record clean so we can live each day, one at a time.

Alateens share on
STEP TEN

I was at school the other day and this guy I had never seen before came up to me and said, "Nice, fake smile."

My first reaction was to get all defensive, but I realized he was right. I was in an awful mood, but I felt I had to smile so everyone would think, "Gee, she doesn't have any problems."

After I thought about it, I realized I do have problems. And there's no reason to hide them or cover them up with a smile. I can only live for myself, and I can only live one day at a time.

✍

There came a time in my life when I had to realize that it was okay for me to make mistakes.

It was difficult for me because I was supposed to be the strong "old-timer" in my Alateen group. I was supposed to be there for everyone else. I thought that for me to make a mistake would mean that I had let everyone else down.

What was really happening is I was realizing that it was time to start taking care of myself again. I am only human. I have the ability to make mistakes. I also have the ability to deal with my mistakes. Fortunately, the benefits of the program are for me too, not just for the newcomer.

Now when I make a mistake I try to admit it as soon as possible. But sometimes I don't do that either. It's okay. I love myself anyway. So does my Higher Power.

✍

I used to sleep so late that I didn't have time for breakfast. I'd jump into my clothes and race right out the door. All the way to school I'd be thinking up excuses to tell my vice principal about why I was late for class. Then I'd get mad at him for making me go to detention.

Of course, I didn't have time to make my lunch in the morning. I almost never had money to buy a lunch. Maybe I could get a candy bar, or else I'd have to mooch a sandwich from one of my friends. Sometimes we'd get in a fight about that.

By the time I got home at night I was hungry enough to pick a fight with my brother. Or else I'd have my mother yell at me for spoiling my dinner. She'd chase me away from the refrigerator to make me wait to eat with everybody else. There was always a lot of arguing and nagging at the table when we were eating. I thought my whole family was crazy.

When my dad went to a treatment center, my brother and I went to Alateen. I heard a kid talk about how much easier his life is since he started eating three meals a day, even if he had to fix all of them for himself. It meant a lot for me to hear him say that. Now the one who tells that story a lot at meetings is me. I know I'm easier to get along with, now that I'm not so hungry all the time.

The first thing I learned in Alateen was that I never had to be alone again. I wish I would have remembered it.

Somehow when my parents' marriage broke up I couldn't understand what was happening to me. Even after so much time in Alateen, I just couldn't quit blaming my parents for wrecking our family and for ruining my life. I forgot that I can only be responsible for me. And I forgot that each of my parents can only be responsible for their individual actions.

When divorce became apparent in our family, it was time for me to look at what knowledge and insight I had gained from this program. It was time for me to take the focus off my parents and to take a look at the good and the bad in me. I had to be willing to improve the good qualities and to work on the bad.

Not surprisingly, however, I chose to focus only on my bad qualities, and I made them worse. I could have saved myself so much trouble if only I had had enough self-respect to take a fresh look at all of my characteristics. I think it's called a daily inventory.

Instead, I became everything I had been before I ever came to Alateen. I forgot to treat my parents' divorce the same way that I'd treated my dad's drinking. I forgot that it wasn't my responsibility to decide whether it was morally right or wrong. I'd learned that my dad didn't drink because he wanted revenge, and that he wasn't doing it out of stupidity. But I didn't apply these same principles to my parents' divorce.

I started feeling very alone again, just like I'd felt before I came to Alateen. I started feeling very afraid of what this situation might bring. I started feeling miserable again, and I started feeling very, very bitter. I knew that some of my fellow Alateen members had gone through what I was going through. But I felt like no one was having the same emotional pain that I was having.

I alienated myself from my family and from my Alateen friends. I claimed I didn't care anymore, but I did care. I tried to hide my negative attitudes behind the divorce, the same way I tried to hide them behind the alcoholic's bottle many years before. Of course, I had the right to feel the way that I felt. But I didn't have the right to push my feelings on other people, just to try to get them to change their minds about something I didn't like. And although it's okay for me to feel whatever I'm feeling, I also know when I hang on to those negative feelings I'll continue to suffer from a lot of emotional pain.

So, finally, I've decided to do Step Ten instead. I'm questioning my own behavior to see if I agree with what I'm doing. At night before I go to sleep, I think about what I've done during the day. Sometimes I know right away if I agree with what I've done. Other times I might have to think about it for a little while.

Nobody tells me what to do. Nobody tells me to do the Tenth Step or any other Step, but I feel a whole lot better when I remind myself to be responsible for me. After everything that has happened in my family, I'm still in Alateen, my dad is in AA, and my mom is in Al-Anon. I wish I could grow in this program by just listening to everybody else's pain. But most of the time I find that the only pain I'm growing through is mine.

Workshop On
STEP TEN

Continued to take personal inventory and when we were wrong promptly admitted it.

Complete the following sentences, adding as many sentences as you want.

When I'm paying attention to my attitudes, I ...

When I'm paying attention to my actions, I ...

When I've made a mistake and I admit it right away, I ...

I know I'm working Step Ten when ...

STEP ELEVEN

Sought through prayer and meditation to improve our conscious contact with God as we understood Him, praying only for knowledge of His will for us and the power to carry that out.

There are many different prayers that we can say and many different ways that we can meditate. All of them can bring us closer to our Higher Power.

Prayer can be anything we say or think. It is a way for us to talk to our Higher Power. By praying frequently during the day we can improve our sense of closeness to our Higher Power. This kind of conscious contact helps us feel that we are not alone. Our Higher Power can be present for us any time and any place. All we need to do is think of the message we would like to send. It can be as brief as, "Hello" or "Thank you" or "I love you." Also, our message can be as long as we would like it to be.

A prayer often used in Alateen and Al-Anon is the Serenity Prayer: "God, grant me the serenity to accept the things I cannot change, courage to change the things I can, and wisdom to know the difference." In this short prayer we acknowledge where serenity and courage and wisdom come from. The Serenity Prayer does not belong to any particular religion, so people from many different religions feel comfortable using it.

If prayer is when we talk to God, then meditation can be like God talking to us. Meditation can take many forms and little messages can come to us while we are trying to concentrate on our meditation. These unplanned messages can be gifts of thoughts or feelings from our Higher Power. Often they sound like very small whispers, gently telling us things that are helpful to know about ourselves.

God, as we understood Him, has to do with our thoughts and feelings about our Higher Power. Our understanding of God does not have to be the same as anyone else's. We can think of God the way we hope deep down in our heart that He, She or It really is.

When we ask only for God's will for us and the power to carry it out, we are asking for wisdom. Most of us realize when we ask God for specific things we do not know what is really good for us. We only know what we really want. When we ask for wisdom, we are asking God to share special knowledge with us. When we are in conscious contact with our Higher Power, all things are possible.

Alateens share on
STEP ELEVEN

When I meditate I imagine that I'm taking a trip inside my head. Along the way during my trip, I encounter black patches of pain, fear and hate, everything I've always tried to deny that I'm feeling. I've denied that I was feeling those things, because if I wasn't feeling them then I wouldn't have to argue or start crying.

Now in my mind I go past all of that pain, fear and hate.

I find a place where a nice, calm, blue sky is spreading over a peaceful field. In this place there is a slight breeze blowing through tall, green grass. In my mind, I call this peaceful place, serenity.

When my father goes into random fits of rage, he screams and shouts and mauls everyone who gets in his way. He takes a perfectly beautiful day and turns it into garbage. I used to think that my father had killed my serenity. Then I discovered that I can find serenity in an Alateen meeting. Now I've discovered that I can find serenity in my own mind.

Every day I try to spend a little time with my eyes closed, picturing a peaceful field where the sky is blue and the breeze is blowing through the grass. I have my serenity again.

✍

I've been hurt and affected by the disease of alcoholism. As a result, I've played crazy mind games with myself. A voice inside my head has told me that I'm bad and stupid and a lot of other things that no one wants to hear. This voice has been hammering away at my brain for so long that I started thinking it was my conscience talking. But it wasn't my conscience. It wasn't even me. It was the voice of an adult in my family who started abusing me when I was two or three years old.

This voice has been so convincing that it's gotten me to punish myself for things that weren't my fault. It's told me that I don't deserve to have fun or to treat myself well, because I'm a bad person. Well, all the harm that I've done to myself is really hard to admit. I've felt depressed and angry at myself. I've even thought that I didn't deserve to live. The craziness and the pain almost took over my life.

If it wasn't for Alateen, I'd still be punishing myself. If it wasn't for Step Eleven, I wouldn't know how good it is for me to be nice to myself. My Higher Power wants me to be happy. All I have to do is find quiet, little, peaceful times during the day so I can listen.

I used to dwell on the past. I always thought about how my life would be different if I had done this or that.

When I got to Alateen I fell in love with the Serenity Prayer. Saying the Serenity Prayer so many times in my mind helped me learn about myself. I learned that I was worrying about the past, even though the past is something that I can't change.

I learned that what I was really doing was wasting my time. I also learned from the Serenity Prayer that there is something that I can change. I can change the present. Especially, in the present I can make decisions that I feel good about. It isn't always easy, but it's possible. Thanks to Alateen, I can live in the here and now.

A friend in an Alateen meeting said, "Prayer is when we talk to God, and meditation is when God talks to us."

That helped me figure out when I was praying and when I was meditating. So far, I've done a whole lot more of the talking part. No wonder it's so hard for me to find out what God's will is for me.

When I'm with my Alateen friends, that's when I'm the happiest. I can forget about all that's bothering me, especially my parents.

Sometimes I hate it when my parents are together because they can strike up an argument so easily. They don't argue about alcohol very much anymore. They just pick at each other. It usually starts as a joke, and then my mom gets defensive and starts yelling, half crying. My dad says she's being unreasonable, so mom stomps out of the room or out of the house.

Because of the Steps, especially Three, Five, Seven, Eleven and Twelve, I realize that I can only change certain things about myself and nothing about the alcoholic. But I've learned that that's okay, because God is backing me up, 100%.

Before I came to Alateen, I felt completely alone. My mom told me that I could talk to her, but she didn't understand that that didn't work for me. I needed kids my own age that I could talk with. I needed other kids of alcoholics.

There's a kind of honesty between us that makes it a lot easier for me to want to get help. When I'm talking at a meeting I don't have to worry about hurting my parents feelings or picking sides in their arguments or making them look bad. It's easier for me to ask for help from my friends and from my Higher Power if I don't have to worry about my parents' reactions while I'm trying to take care of myself.

Alateen showed me that it's okay to be vulnerable and that it's okay to have feelings. I don't have to be tough all the time. Alateen also showed me that my Higher Power can be a forgiving and loving God and that He isn't cruel and mean.

There are times when I still need to be reminded that my Higher Power will always be there as long as I allow Him to be. My Higher Power is the only reason I've been able to deal with rape, gangs and suicide.

I pray. I call my sponsor. I talk with other Alateens. I change what I can, and I let the rest go. I continue to pray and hope for whatever God feels needs to be done in my life. And today I know I'm not alone.

✍

My favorite meditation is to close my eyes and count each time I breathe out. I count each time I breathe out until I count up to four, then I start over again.

Pretty soon my mind starts to wander. As soon as I realize that I'm thinking about other things, then I remind myself to start counting again. When I'm reminding myself I try to be gentle. It doesn't work if I yell at myself in my mind, or if I give myself a hard time. All I have to do is to start counting each time I breathe out until I count up to four. Then I start counting all over again.

If I can meditate like this every day for about five minutes, I feel calm and relaxed. Then it feels like God is in charge of my life, not me.

✍

One of my prayers that I say every day is a list of things that I ask God to help me to accept and to take care of for me.

God, please accept me — my life and my willpower and my feelings, my abilities and all of my ambitions, my self-esteem and all of my dreams, my school-work and all my sports and all of my friends, my sexuality and all of my special relationships, my fears and all of my sadness and all of my sorrows, my pleasures and all of my joys, my failures and all of my successes and all of my hopes — into Your loving care. Grant me knowledge of Your will for me and the power to carry it out.

Some days I say this prayer many times. Other days I only say it once, at night on my knees at the side of my bed.

I have believed in God (my Higher Power) nearly all my life. There was a phase I went through when my life was so bad that I thought there wasn't a God to help me.

I now know that my mum has a disease and that it's not God's fault. From hearing Alateens share at meetings, I know my life could have been a lot worse than it was. So now I know that my Higher Power is helping me.

Being in Alateen, I now talk to God in the way that I want to. If I have a problem, I talk to my Higher Power as though He is a friend, like He has a shoulder for me to cry on. Sometimes I do cry, and it makes me feel a lot better.

I turn to my Higher Power nearly always when I'm in bed, sometimes when I'm on the bus or when I'm walking along the side of the road. I think about Him when I'm not doing anything in particular, when I've some time on my hands. Nearly every time when something good happens I think about God, and I thank Him.

When I'm in bed at night talking to my Higher Power, I only talk about being upset because of something that's gone wrong. But by constantly talking to my Higher Power, for whatever reason, I feel like my relationship with Him is getting stronger and stronger.

Workshop On
STEP ELEVEN

Sought through prayer and meditation to improve our conscious contact with God as we understood Him, praying only for knowledge of His will for us and the power to carry that out.

Complete the following sentences, adding as many sentences as you want.

When I talk with God, I...

To me, meditation means ...

To me, conscious contact with God means...

When I ask God to let me know what He wants for me, I ...

Asking God to give me power to carry out what He wants for me, lets me...

STEP TWELVE

Having had a spiritual awakening as the result of these Steps, we tried to carry this message to others, and to practice these principles in all our affairs.

Many of us entered Alateen with a broken spirit. By working the first eleven Steps we gradually came to feel more and more alive. Now we are aware of how much better we feel, and we want to share what we have experienced. We want to let people know that we used to feel downhearted, but now we feel full of gratitude and hope. It does not mean that we will no longer have any problems. It means when problems come up we feel confident that things will work out all right.

The change in our spirit did not happen overnight. It did not come without a certain amount of commitment and work on our part, but we also did not have to do it alone. We had the benefit of our group and our Higher Power. We had sponsors and friends. We had the support of all of Alateen and Al-Anon. And now we want to play a bigger role in offering that support to others.

So, now do we speak for all of Alateen? Do we advise others to do exactly what we have done? Do we make promises about what the program can do for everyone in every painful situation all around the world?

Of course, we do not. In fact, we continue to do exactly what we have always done. We share our experience, strength and hope. So, how are things different now? Things may not be different, but we are different. We let people know what Alateen has done for us. We volunteer. Wherever we are and whatever we are doing we are carrying the message. Even when we are far away from any kind of Alateen activity, we are still carrying the message of hope for all to see. By practicing these principles in all our affairs, we are sharing our new spirit with everyone we contact.

Alateens share on
STEP TWELVE

Before I joined Alateen I went to a couple of open Al-Anon meetings and anniversaries with my mother. I thought they were pretty boring. But then there were a couple of occasions when I heard an Alateen speaker talking. I thought, "Wow, he has the same experiences that I have."

When I saw teenagers like me up there talking in front of all those people, I never thought I would ever do that. The idea of talking about my own experiences, telling personal thoughts and feelings, seemed about as likely as me playing in the Super Bowl.

Today, however, I've done it. Sure, it was scary. All I did was talk the same way I've been talking at my own Alateen meeting. I have some more invitations to speak at AA and Al-Anon meetings. I'll read some literature and talk to my sponsor, my home group, and then I'll go do it again.

✍

Without the Alateen program I was very shy. I felt like I was the only flower in a meadow full of thistles and grass and weeds. Now I feel like a young tree in a forest full of protection and good friends.

I'm not too shy to reach out for help when I need it now. And more and more I'm feeling strong enough to help someone else. I'm very grateful for all the help I've gotten in Alateen, and I want to be there for the next kid who feels as lost as I used to feel. Maybe someday I'll even become an Alateen sponsor.

✍

A gift of sponsoring other girls is that I have learned to have compassion, forgiveness and love for my family. My brother and sisters don't go to meetings anymore and that used to bother me a whole lot. But I have learned this program is not for people who need it, but for people who want it. And I want it! This program is for me and I get to keep coming back no matter what! God continues to put girls in my life who remind me of my sisters. My love for them and the love for my sisters increases. I get to practice acceptance and detachment. Most of all, in practicing the Twelfth Step which is sponsorship, I continue to pass this program on so that maybe one day if anyone in my family comes back, it will be here just as it was for me.

✍

Three of us Alateens accepted an invitation to speak at a school not too far from our area. At first the idea was pretty scary. We were supposed to go class to class. Each of us would talk, and then we'd take questions from the students. Some of the questions had nothing to do with Alateen. Some asked, "How old are you?" Others said, "What are you doing Saturday night?" A few even turned out to be serious questions about alcoholic situations in a family.

After awhile it got easier to talk. I'm glad I did it. I don't think I'll be quite so nervous the next time.

I've found people in the Alateen program who love me for who I am and who understand what I've been through. I also have a God of my understanding who has brought me a long way.

I don't want to make it sound like I went out to a field on a nice summer day and caught all of this with a big net.

I had to put all of my energy and effort into the Twelve Steps for anything to work. I'm just glad that it works. I know one way to make sure it keeps working for me — I have to keep giving it away, every chance I get.

When I was eleven years old I got into a lot of problems with my family and friends. Then my grandmother came up to me and told me about Alateen. It sounded like it might be okay, so I said I would go and see if I liked it.

Well, when I walked through the door I was greeted by a bunch of people who came up to me and said, "I love you." And they hugged me. It really shocked me. I sat through the meeting without saying anything. I held all of my feelings inside, but I listened a lot. That night after the meeting I went home and cried myself to sleep. It really scared me the way those people talked because it was as if they had been reading a book about my life.

I kept coming back, and eventually I talked. It felt really good to get off my chest all of the things that I'd been carrying around inside of me for years. When I talked it felt like all of those people really listened to me. And it felt like they cared about me. I keep coming back for two reasons. One is to keep getting the caring and sharing of the program. The other is to help newcomers feel the same way I did when the Alateens listened to me that first night when I started talking about the truth in my life.

I've been in Alateen for about seven years now. A year ago I had a terrible experience. I thought I didn't need to go to Alateen meetings anymore.

I felt like I didn't have any of the problems people were sharing because my mom was in AA and doing fine. All the things I shared seemed irrelevant to what everyone else was going through.

Then, with the help of my sponsor and a friend in the program, I realized that I needed Alateen more than anything. I'm grateful to Alateen because it has given me so much. Through Alateen I've learned a lot about myself and the alcoholic in my life. I'm also learning that you get out of the program what you give. So I'm giving more now, and I'm feeling even better than I did before.

✎

I have lived with an alcoholic for my entire life. It's made many things very difficult, including schoolwork and social activities. Before Alateen I felt very embarrassed by the topic of alcoholics or alcoholism. In fact, after my first Alateen meeting I didn't come back for over two months. Since then I've continued to go to meetings, and now I even accept invitations to go to other schools to talk about my own experiences.

I tell kids that whenever someone used to talk about alcoholism in my classes at school I always got real quiet or else I cried. To this day I can tell when kids have alcoholism in their homes. Usually they get real quiet, like I did, or else they get hyper and obnoxious. I remember how awful I felt about what was happening in my home. I wish I could have had the courage to talk to my teachers about it.

I wish they could have told me about Alateen or counseling or a variety of other things. Some people may think that I talk about Alateen for the attention I get, but that's not the reason. I talk about my life because it helps me live with it. And I like the idea that it might help somebody else who might be just as scared as I used to be.

✎

When I was a freshman I noticed that some of my friends had parents who suffered from alcoholism. I invited them to come with me to my Alateen meeting. When their parents found out, they refused to let my friends go.

I wondered if we could start an Alateen meeting at school during the day, so I started a petition among all of the students in our school. To my surprise, a lot of kids signed the petition. In fact, almost three-quarters of my school signed it.

The principal gave us permission. Two Al-Anon adults agreed to be our sponsors. Fifty kids showed up at the first meeting. Now we have several sessions during the week, and a lot of kids go.

I remember searching for love. I searched for it in boyfriends and other friends. I especially looked for it in members of my own family. But I never felt love until I found Alateen.

The love that I found in Alateen is unlike anything that I've ever expected. It's very special but it doesn't come from other people. They showed it to me, but they didn't give it to me.

That special kind of love comes from inside of myself. I learned how to love me. In the Twelve Steps it's called a spiritual awakening. But what it really means to me is that I am a very valuable and lovable person. The whole world changed for me in Alateen. I felt my spirit awaken. My spirit is awake now, because I love myself.

When my dad died I lost all hope. Then when my mom joined AA she told me about Alateen. Alateen has given me my life back.

I've never seen so much love between so many people. I've never had so many friends in my whole life. Alateen is the best thing that ever happened to me. If it can help me, it can help anyone — even somebody who has already given up hope, like I had.

I never thought I would experience a spiritual awakening. Then one day I was walking in my special place, along the edge of a beautiful lake, surrounded by trees. I sat down and started noticing the ducks and the geese.

They looked so serene, the way they glided across the water. I started singing, just enjoying myself and the sound of my own voice. I felt very peaceful. Pretty soon I noticed all of these ducks and geese swimming toward me. They came ashore and started preening themselves and getting comfortable.

As they relaxed, surrounding me in a semi-circle, I started to feel like I was a performer and they were my audience. As they lay down, watching me and listening to me, I started to feel like I was an angel.

Gradually, I began to realize that God had given me some very special gifts. I think I started to appreciate myself in a whole new way that day. I was singing to ducks and geese, and I was feeling special. Ever since that day I have sensed an ability I have to be a soothing influence on myself and on the people around me.

I've learned our Alateen group has a lot of love. I could feel it the first meeting I went to.

I walked in the door, unsure of what to expect. There were smiling faces and cheery voices. My best friend (who brought me there) was hugging everyone, including boys. I didn't know what to think of it.

As the meeting progressed, I began to understand. Even though I didn't know these people, I could feel the closeness that passed between them. I could feel it when they were offering that same kind of closeness to me. I had heard that there was a certain kind of love at these places, but I never felt anything like it until my first night in Alateen.

I'm not surprised now to see wide eyes and confused faces when new people walk into our Alateen meeting. Except now I'm part of the closeness that's here. I always want to be ready to pass on a warm welcome to the newcomers, the same way someone gave it to me when I was new.

Workshop On
STEP TWELVE

Having had a spiritual awakening as the result of these Steps, we tried to carry this message to others, and to practice these principles in all our affairs.

Complete the following sentences, adding as many sentences as you want.

A spiritual awakening to me means ...

I realized I had had a spiritual awakening when ...

When I look at all the ways my life has changed since I came into Alateen, I believe ...

Carrying the Alateen message to others means ...

When I practice the Alateen ideas and attitudes in my everyday life, I...

INTRODUCTION TO THE TWELVE TRADITIONS

Growing up in an alcoholic family affects each of us in many different ways. Many of us learn to keep secrets. We learn to think badly of people, especially ourselves. And we learn to hide our real feelings.

But, in Alateen we learn a whole different way to treat one another and ourselves. Many of us notice a difference at our very first Alateen meeting. We heard Alateen members talking more honestly and openly than we ever heard anyone talk; we noticed the difference. We see Alateens share their laughter and their tears. And soon we feel *ourselves* starting to laugh or cry with them. We know we've found a place that's very special.

Alateens are special people. What makes Alateens and Alateen so special? The Twelve Steps are what make us special as individuals. But what makes Alateen so special is the way we begin to understand ourselves — and *each other*.

The Twelve Traditions of Alateen are the guidelines that help us learn how to do what we've always wanted to do to become all we are capable of being. The Twelve Traditions show us how to work with others. And more important than just having friends, they teach us how to be a friend. We read the Traditions and share about them at meetings and soon we discover that they have become a very important part of our lives, both inside and outside of meetings.

On the following pages, members of Alateen share their experience, strength, and hope about the Twelve Traditions. We can use their sharings to help us learn more about the Traditions and ourselves. At the end of each section on a Tradition we can express ourselves, if we choose to — just like we do at our Alateen meetings.

ALATEEN'S TWELVE TRADITIONS

Our group experience suggests that the unity of the Alateen Groups depends upon our adherence to these Traditions:

1. Our common welfare should come first; personal progress for the greatest number depends upon unity.

2. For our group purpose there is but one authority — a loving God as He may express Himself in our group conscience. Our leaders are but trusted servants; they do not govern.

3. The only requirement for membership is that there be a problem of alcoholism in a relative or friend. The teenage relatives of alcoholics, when gathered together for mutual aid, may call themselves an Alateen Group provided that, as a group, they have no other affiliation.

4. Each group should be autonomous, except in matters affecting other Alateen and Al-Anon Family Groups or AA as a whole.

5. Each Alateen Group has but one purpose: to help other teenagers of alcoholics. We do this by practicing the Twelve Steps of AA ourselves and by encouraging and understanding the members of our immediate families.

6. Alateens, being part of Al-Anon Family Groups, ought never endorse, finance or lend our name to any outside enterprise, lest problems of money, property and prestige divert us from our primary spiritual aim. Although a separate entity, we should always cooperate with Alcoholics Anonymous.

7. Every group ought to be fully self-supporting, declining outside contributions.

8. Alateen Twelfth Step work should remain forever nonprofessional, but our service centers may employ special workers.

9. Our groups, as such, ought never be organized; but we may create service boards   or committees directly responsible to those they serve.

10. The Alateen Groups have no opinion on outside issues; hence our name ought never be drawn into public controversy.

11. Our public relations policy is based on attraction rather than promotion; we need always maintain personal anonymity at the level of press, radio, TV and films. We need guard with special care the anonymity of all AA members.

12. Anonymity is the spiritual foundation of all our Traditions, ever reminding us to place principles above personalities.

Alateens share on
THE TWELVE TRADITIONS IN GENERAL

I greatly appreciate the Alateen Traditions because every time I go to an Alateen meeting there might be a newcomer needing help.

I practice the Traditions through respecting the newcomers and the longtime members' anonymity, and why they are in our group. If the Alateen Traditions were not followed, there wouldn't be an Alateen. There might be fear and resentment toward each member of the group. The personal stories we tell in Alateen are for the group's ears only; therefore, it is important that the Traditions be practiced in everyone's life as well as in the group.

✍

Our group has come up with a Traditions list for group problem solving:

1. Group conscience vs. opinions of leaders and strong personalities - Traditions One, Two and Twelve.

2. Dominance and strong personalities - Traditions One, Two, Five, and Twelve.

3. Getting off track with outside issues/Purpose of our being in Alateen - Traditions Three, Five and Six.

4. Controversy vs. harmony - Traditions Three, Four, Six, Seven, Eight and Ten.

5. Teachers, monarchs, dictators, gurus, or presidents vs. trusted servants - Traditions One, Two, Nine, Ten, Eleven and Twelve.

6. Conflicts among individuals — autonomy, purpose, unity and principles above personalities — Traditions One, Two, Four and Twelve.

All these solutions to problems come up throughout the year and we try to have a meeting every now and then on this list.

✍

All of the Traditions combined make for a very strong glue that holds the group together. Recently Traditions One and Two have been at the forefront of our group. It's so easy for those of us who have been around for a few meetings to take over a group and to dominate or control it. A lot of times newer members don't care about group decisions and would rather that older members "just do it." This can create an atmosphere for the group's unity to be shattered. It can also permit a few members to become the group's Higher Power or the group's sponsors to take over and run things as they think best.

If one Alateen or Al-Anon member governs or bosses the group, sooner or later the effects will show up and our primary purpose will be pushed in the shadows.

When every member remains aware of the Traditions and their own individual responsibility to participate in the group, the power stays where it really should be — with a loving God, who knows what is best for the group at all times!

Our group reads the Traditions at each meeting and, even if we don't realize it, the repetition places the Traditions in our minds and keeps them fresh.

TRADITION ONE

Our common welfare should come first; personal progress for the greatest number depends upon unity.

Many of us felt surprised by the openness and honesty that we found at our first Alateen meeting. The members who volunteered to share their First Step stories with us said things we thought they would be too afraid to say. While they spoke, everyone listened quietly and respectfully.

Eventually we took the opportunity to speak, too. Although it was hard at first, we managed to say a little about why we came to Alateen. The most amazing part was how everyone paid attention to what we said. It felt like what we were talking about was important too. Then we realized that everyone in Alateen is important.

Alateens stick together. We discuss things together. We make decisions together.

It is our responsibility to keep our meetings safe and on track. Everyone deserves a chance to express an opinion about what goes on, but everyone needs to agree that what the group decides is what will happen. Tradition One means that the group is more important than any individual. Hopefully, each individual is willing to accept what the group decides.

Alateens share on
TRADITION ONE

Our Alateen sponsor mentioned that our group might want to start studying the Traditions. At first, we really weren't too excited about her idea. We thought studying the Traditions might be a little boring.

Someone volunteered to lead a topic meeting on Tradition One. We had so many questions that it turned out to be one of the best meetings our group ever had. What we didn't realize was how much our personal progress depended upon the unity of our group.

✍️

The most important way my Alateen group has helped me is by listening to me. No matter what I say, nobody interrupts or laughs at me or makes negative comments the way they always do at home.

✍️

I used to feel rejected because people put me down—so I learned to keep to myself, so they couldn't hurt me any more.

When I came to Alateen I didn't open up very much. I didn't want people to judge me, and I didn't want anyone to put me down again. But one night at an Alateen meeting it all came tumbling out. I found myself crying for the first time in a long, long time.

The love and support that I got that night from the Alateens in my group gave me the warmest feelings that I have ever felt. Since then my life has changed a lot. I don't feel afraid to be myself anymore. And I don't feel like everyone is going to put me down for who I am.

Today I'm learning more and more about the unconditional love and peace and wisdom of the Alateen program, so maybe I can even pass them on to someone else in the future.

✍️

When I first came to Alateen I wasn't used to people paying any attention when I talked, so I kept quiet — but I listened while other kids spilled their guts. Everybody listened. I couldn't believe it. Finally, I just had to try it myself. So I did.

It feels good when somebody really listens to what I have to say!

I even cried in my group, and sometimes other people cried while I was talking and crying. Nobody ever did that for me before. The Alateen members had feelings for me and were actually crying with me. I wish my mom could do that.

✍️

Growth, to me, is the best part of the Alateen program. That's what I didn't have before. When I met Alateens for the first time they were happy and carefree, but I wasn't. I wanted what they had, and I was determined to get it.

They took me into their group, and pretty soon it was my group, too. Now I've been in the program for over three years. I get to watch all the newcomers grow. It's neat. It's not like if I keep them out I'll have more for myself. It doesn't work that way. We're all in this together, and there's plenty of good stuff for everybody. It's great!

I came to Alateen for the first time three years ago. I was very angry and very depressed. At my first meeting I didn't say a word. After the meeting was over I went home and cried. I hadn't cried in a long time. It felt good.

I'm a much happier person than I was three years ago. Now when I'm upset or having a problem I know how to deal with it. I know that somebody in Alateen is always there for me.

The first time I experienced unconditional love was at an Alateen mini-convention. It was a great experience. Unconditional love means to get love without having to do anything for it. It also means to give love without expecting to get anything back.

Growing up in an alcoholic home, I always gave love and demanded to get it back. Or else my family gave me love, and I didn't want to give anything back. Either way, I got hurt. At the Alateen convention, we did this exercise where you know that you don't have to give anything back. It really feels great. I'm glad that I participated. It gave me a great feeling of unity with all of the other Alateens. I would tell anyone to try it if they get the chance.

Everyone in my Alateen group is important, because we really help each other to feel better. Talking about my experiences really helps me. So does listening to other people talk.

I even think what I say can help somebody else. It sure feels like it can. When I see the looks on people's faces when I talk, it really makes me feel like I'm helping.

✍

Before Alateen, I was an island. I felt separated from everyone around me. Trying to talk to my peers and family was like putting a message in a bottle and hoping someone would find it and understand.

When I came to Alateen, the members refused to allow me to isolate. They welcomed me like I was an old friend. I felt important and worthy of love for the first time. This love was a foundation on which to build my recovery.

In Alateen, I have never felt alone. Whenever I've reached out for help, the loving hand of the program has always been there. Thanks, everyone. It really works.

✍

When times were tough at home I did a dumb thing. I ran away. When I was on the run I was afraid to let my Alateen friends know what I was doing. I was afraid that they would bounce me right out of the group. The truth accidentally slipped out at a meeting one night, but they didn't toss me out. Instead, all of them said that they could relate. They said that they had felt the same way that I was feeling.

I got plenty of hugs that night and even a small kiss on my forehead from an older member. It always was a problem for me to trust people. Now I know there are plenty of people I can trust.

For a long time, there was some uneasiness in our group. We knew that we were having problems due to cliques, but were afraid to ever bring it up at a business meeting. Finally, our Alateen sponsor suggested we use the Group Inventory sheet and take a "A Group Inventory" at our next meeting — this helped. One of the younger members got the courage to say how it hurt her when she felt left out during the break, or after a meeting when certain kids stayed together, talked and hung out together. Her honesty made our group members realize that Alateen doesn't shut anyone out — we're all family.

What came out of this business meeting was a suggestion to read Tradition One. The younger member was asked to read a sharing on Tradition One and what we remembered was the word "unity." It helped us to see that if we as a group allow cliques to exist, then we really aren't practicing unity. Alateen is our family and being affected by the disease of alcoholism brings us together in unity.

The disease of alcoholism brought us into the program and Tradition One keeps us united as a group. Each member is the special part that makes up the whole. Unity is like a circle connecting each person and cliques are like broken circles. Today our group knows that if we want cliques we can have them outside of the circle of love that unites our Alateen group. We are one group, one circle of love.

Workshop On
TRADITION ONE

Our common welfare should come first; personal progress for the greatest number depends upon unity.

Complete the following sentences, adding as many sentences as you want.

The common welfare of my Alateen group means ...

Our common welfare should come first because ...

My personal progress in Alateen means that I ...

My personal progress in Alateen depends on group unity because ...

I do my part in maintaining group unity by ...

TRADITION TWO

For our group purpose there is but one authority — a loving God as He may express Himself in our group conscience. Our leaders are but trusted servants; they do not govern.

Alateen is a fellowship of equals. When it is time to make a decision, everyone has a right to speak and everyone has a right to vote. Even a voice that disagrees with the majority can add insight and understanding to the discussion. When everyone has had a chance to talk, then the group decides by majority vote. We call this process the group conscience.

In Alateen our trusted servants do not make the decisions. They have the same right to speak that everyone else has. Along with the senior members, they may guide the group according to their understanding of the Twelve Traditions, but when the time comes for a decision, the vote of the group is what counts. The responsibility of the group's leaders is to carry out what the group decides.

Alateens share on
TRADITION TWO

Tradition Two is one of the Traditions our group studies when group problems arise. In this Tradition, it states that the one authority is a loving God who expresses Himself through our group conscience. Our Alateen group talks about problems we might have in our group, allowing each individual to speak about their experience or opinion. Then, as a group, we vote on the direction we will go. The second part of the Tradition states that our leaders are trusted servants and do not govern. I have spent a lot of time thinking about the difference between leading and governing. I believe when I chair a meeting I need to be a good leader. If the voice of the group leads to a potential problem or dangerous decision, I need to speak about my fears. Today, I can do that by sharing my experience and voicing my concern. Then, with an informed group conscience, the God of my understanding will be a part of the decision making. A solution can be reached with everyone feeling they are involved with the process.

✍

Before I started reading the Twelve Steps and the Twelve Traditions I wanted to know, "Who runs this place? Who owns Alateen?" Until I started working my own program, I thought, "Someone else must be in charge of my program — and of me."

Alateen was my very first experience for me to be in charge of myself; at home I wasn't; at school and church I wasn't. I still have trouble working the Steps and Traditions, but it's becoming clearer to me what the difference is between Alateen and the other parts of my life. In Alateen the only authority, besides me, is my Higher Power.

When I work my program there's no reason for me to have to work it alone, either. My Higher Power helps me. Our leaders help me too, but they don't order me around. At first it was a real shock, being treated like an equal by so many people. But I'm getting used to it now. I especially like it when a problem comes up in our meeting and somebody says to me, "What do you think?"

The thing that hurt me the most was living with my brother. He was the brother from another planet. He acted like a military dictator.

My brother ruled my life until I came into Alateen. I've resented him for a long, long time. But in Alateen I'm learning to forgive him. Today my Higher Power is in charge of my life. My brother isn't. My sponsor isn't. No one in the program tries to tell me what to do. I'm trying to get used to not having a boss.

✍

Sometimes we have members of our group who are not willing to listen. They disrupt the meeting by giving advice or by making funny remarks. They might interrupt someone who is speaking, or when it is their turn to speak they might have little or nothing to share.

At these times, those of us who have been in the program for a while know that the disruptive member is probably hurting. We may even remember what it was like when we felt like doing the same things.

None of us is in charge of anyone else. Each of us is in charge of our own recovery. But sometime during the meeting or in private we might share a little bit of our experience with the one who is being disruptive. We might even remember to mention something that worked when someone shared their experience, strength, and hope with us a long time ago. It works when we work it.

✍

We have a different member chair our meetings each week. One time, we had a chairperson who got on a power trip. In the meeting she only picked her friends to share, and she wouldn't let anyone else say anything. Some people left the meeting feeling hurt because they didn't get a chance to talk.

Since I'm the group representative, I went to our sponsor and asked what to do about the situation. He suggested that I ask the chairperson to lead a meeting on Tradition Two. Boy, did that work. Tradition Two says that everyone is important and that the chairpersons of meetings guide the group, but they don't control the group. Now the only expert in our meetings is our Higher Power.

About a year ago, when I was still the treasurer for my group, we had a group conscience meeting to decide if we wanted to add an extra sponsor to our group. We talked about whether or not we should allow this man to join us.

Personally, I liked the guy, so I wanted him to be accepted. When our discussion seemed to be in his favor, I asked for a vote.

Looking back on what I did, I now believe that I was in violation of Tradition Two, "Our leaders are but trusted servants, they do not govern." By asking for a vote when I did, I was pushing the issue in a way that suited me, not the group.

My mistake was the idea that I was supposed to be in control, just because I was on the steering committee. In forcing the issue, I took the end result out of God's hands and I put it into mine.

I'm sorry I did the wrong thing. Next time I'll try to do better.

I was in Alateen for a long time but didn't do anything. One night after our group hadn't met for six months, we got a new sponsor. She said we needed to have a group representative (GR), secretary and treasurer. So I volunteered to be the GR. I didn't have any idea about what to do, but over the one year period, I got the idea. I was lucky that my sponsor was the GR of her Al-Anon group, so she knew all about it. I went with her to the district meetings and area assembly.

I know that Alateen groups need good leadership. I'm glad I tried it. It helps me get a grip on how to work with the group and it helps me grow in the program.

God has a funny way of making good things happen in our group conscience meetings. As long as the teens who have been in the program the longest don't try to use the group conscience to fit their own mold, eventually everything works out okay.

In many instances my group has had problems and a group conscience was taken. Some of the greatest thoughts and feelings have come out of this. I think our group really comes together during these special, group conscience discussions.

Our Alateen group is a school group, so every year we have elections right after we return from summer break. The last time we elected officers I sensed a certain amount of tension among the members because of the individuals we elected — but we were the ones who elected them.

Anyway, before too long we felt like our trusted servants were not doing a good enough job. For example, both our group representative and our alternate group representative weren't even showing up for regular meetings. They didn't show up for district meetings or for conventions, either.

We decided to call a group conscience meeting to discuss the situation. Of course we were all a little nervous at first, because we felt that maybe they thought we were kicking them out of our group. It just so happened that the people we'd elected didn't want their positions, anyway. So we had new elections — and now everyone is happier than they were before, and we are a much healthier Alateen group because of what we went through.

Workshop On
TRADITION TWO

For our group purpose there is but one authority — a loving God as He may express Himself in our group conscience. Our leaders are but trusted servants; they do not govern.

Complete the following sentences, adding as many sentences as you want.

A group conscience is ...

I participate in a group conscience by ...

My loving God expresses himself by ...

"Our leaders are but trusted servants; they do not govern" — to me this actually means ...

A trusted servant in Alateen can ...

A trusted servant in Alateen should not ...

I can use Tradition Two in my ...

I can show I am a trusted servant by ...

TRADITION THREE

The only requirement for membership is that there be a problem of alcoholism in a relative or friend. The teenage relatives of alcoholics, when gathered together for mutual aid, may call themselves an Alateen Group provided that, as a group, they have no other affiliation.

If someone else's drinking has ever affected us, we are eligible for membership in Alateen. We might not be living with the person. We might not be friends with him or her, anymore. The person may no longer be living. We are eligible to join Alateen when we realize that someone else's drinking has affected us.

The way we join Alateen is we start coming to meetings. If there isn't an Alateen meeting near us we can start one or attend a local Al-Anon meeting and ask for a member to help us start a group. Alateen guidelines for starting and conducting meetings are always available through the local Al-Anon information service or by writing the Al-Anon World Service Office.

Alateen meetings are often held in churches, schools or other facilities. The reason is because people at these places are nice enough to rent meeting rooms to us. Alateen is not a part of any of these organizations. We appreciate the chance to rent their meeting room, but that is our only connection with them.

Alateens share on
TRADITION THREE

I guess I never wanted to face the truth about what was happening in my family. I knew my father had a problem, but I didn't know what kind of a problem it was. I knew that there was abuse, especially verbal and mental abuse. Sometimes it would hurt so bad that I wished my dad would just knock me out so it would be over with, quickly.

Now that I've been in Alateen for awhile, I realize that the problem is alcoholism. I've also come to realize that there's a safe place where I can belong. I thank my Higher Power every day for my Alateen group. Alateen is my new family.

✍

The Alateens have helped me cope with problems that I couldn't cope with by myself, or with anyone else. I came from a family that had divorce, deaths, alcoholism, drugs, and incest. I felt very embarrassed about my family before I came to Alateen. Actually, I felt humiliated.

When I was thirteen years old I was very nearly raped by my neighbor. My grandparents died while my mom and my stepfather were getting a divorce. As a result of all this, I was feeling so bad about myself that I wanted to be dead. Instead, I thank God for bringing me to Alateen.

I also thank God for giving me the strength to share my horrid past with all of these beautiful people. All I needed to join Alateen was to have a problem of alcoholism in a relative or a friend. The same things that I was so embarrassed about have actually made it possible for me to get the help that I need.

✍

I live in a group home so I don't really have any family around. But I don't have to live with an alcoholic to belong in Alateen. All I have to have is a problem of alcoholism in a relative or a friend.

✍

I feel very relieved because some good can finally come out of my mother's drinking. If it wasn't for her drinking, then I couldn't be a member of Alateen.

It's funny how I've always been afraid that people would find out about my mom. But in Alateen it's no big deal. I'm just like everybody else.

✍

We were a middle class family of five. My role was that of "little mommy." I was very busy telling my two younger brothers what they should do and what they should not do.

The older of the two boys played the role of "the rebel" — loud, rude and openly defiant. His role was quite different from the goody-two-shoes behavior that I practiced. The younger brother was "the brat." He could get away with things we couldn't, because we "should know better."

My mother was "the martyr." She was obsessed with how many cans of beer my dad drank. It seemed like she couldn't do anything right, while she was sacrificing everything for the family. Dad's themes were, "I-can-drink-as-well-as-the-next-guy," and "besides, so-and-so drinks more like an alcoholic than I do." And Dad was never wrong about anything.

Our whole family was addicted to television. Most of our conversations took place during the commercials. We didn't know how to communicate with each other at all. I only realized some of the effects that alcoholism has had on our family after I went to Alateen. I heard stories of other kids who came from situations similar to the kinds of situations I'd been in. We shared similar feelings, even though some of the details of our lives were different. After attending Alateen for a while, I got a sponsor so I could learn to use the Twelve Steps in my daily living. My sponsor has been able to help me by sharing personal stories, giving good suggestions, and by just listening.

As a result of all the help I've gotten in my program, I've come to a better understanding of myself and the role that alcoholism has played in my life. At first, my family tiptoed to the car to go to our meetings, so Dad wouldn't find out. Eventually though, everything came out in the open. Now we're learning to face the facts of our disease.

✍

Before my dad checked himself into an alcoholism treatment center I had no hope. I felt like my world was ending.

There never was any kind of hope in my family. Hope didn't come from my father's treatment center either, or even from his recovery — not really. Hope is what I got by coming to Alateen.

Hope is just the most awesome feeling. To know that so many good things have happened for members whose families used to be just like mine is the best feeling I've ever had. In Alateen, instead of my life feeling like it's ending, it feels like it's just begun.

My little brother is an alcoholic and he has the toughest time growing up in my family. He has the most to overcome, yet he gets the least amount of help from my folks.

I've had plenty of other reasons to come into the program, but he's one of the reasons that I keep coming back. I know if I don't keep getting help for myself, then I'll have to settle for the same kind of treatment that my brother gets from our folks at home.

When people don't know any better, it's easy to see how they can get lost. Now that I do know a better way to live, I can't imagine why I'd ever want to go back to the way things used to be. When I get out of Alateen, I plan on going right into Al-Anon.

Workshop On
TRADITION THREE

The only requirement for membership is that there be a problem of alcoholism in a relative or friend. The teenage relatives of alcoholics, when gathered together for mutual aid, may call themselves an **Alateen Group** provided that, as a group, they have no other affiliation.

Complete the following sentences, adding as many sentences as you want.

People who can attend Alateen are ...

It is important that only teenage relatives and friends of alcoholics attend Alateen because ...

If my Alateen group joined a sports league, we would be violating this Tradition because ...

To me affiliation means ...

Alateen groups should not have outside affiliations because ...

TRADITION FOUR

Each group should be autonomous, except in matters affecting other Alateen and Al-Anon Family Groups or AA as a whole.

Tradition Four recognizes the independence of each Alateen group. We set our own meeting times and choose our own meeting format. We elect leaders and raise the money to pay our expenses. We pay rent for our meeting room, buy our own literature and decide whether to have refreshments. It is necessary for us to have an adult Al-Anon member to sponsor our group, but it is our decision whether to accept the Al-Anon member who volunteered. If we want a different sponsor, we need to ask for one.

Our group can decide to play as active a role as we want in all Alateen and Al-Anon activities. By sending our representatives to district or information service meetings our group will have one vote, along with all of the other Alateen and Al-Anon groups. By sending our representative to the area assemblies, we can have a vote to pick the delegate for the World Service Conference. We also have a voice by letting our delegate know what our needs are.

Alateens share on
TRADITION FOUR

When we say our Alateen group is autonomous, it means that we make our own decisions—but we can't make decisions for any other group. For example, one of my Alateen meetings allows members to leave the room at any time during a meeting. Another meeting has a five-minute break in the middle of the meeting, but at any other time nobody is supposed to leave the room. Both meetings are right, but neither meeting can tell the other meeting what to do.

✍️

I didn't feel safe when I first came to Alateen because I didn't know what was expected of me. But the first thing the Alateens did at the meeting was to read the Twelve Steps and the Twelve Traditions. Right away I started learning how much I was going to be involved in all of the decisions that affected my group.

Even after I heard all the guidelines I didn't think we'd ever follow them, but we do. I've never felt this safe anywhere. I really like having so much to say about what we do in our meetings.

✍️

At our Alateen meeting, we have a speaker at our group on the first Monday of each month. A while ago, someone from another state attended on the same night as our speaker meeting. He went to Alateen before he moved to our town. When he came to our meeting he said his old group didn't have speakers come to the meetings, and he wanted to know if that was allowed. Our sponsor told us that Tradition Four says that each group can decide what they feel is best for them as long as it doesn't break the other Traditions or hurt other groups like AA, Al-Anon, or another group of Alateen.

At my Alateen meeting we sometimes have people who aren't teenagers come to the door and ask if they can join us. Usually, one of us or our sponsor asks them why they want to attend our meeting. Then we ask them to wait out in the hall while we take a vote.

If they are kids younger than thirteen, they're usually very surprised when we vote yes, that they can join our meeting. But we almost always vote yes. I think it's neat to be the one who goes out in the hall to tell someone that we've voted them into our meeting — the look on their face is really special. They always come into the room smiling, as though they feel especially welcome.

The only reason that we might vote no for kids younger than thirteen is if our group is pretty old, like seventeen and eighteen and nineteen year-olds—then we suggest that real young kids might try another meeting. It's just that what we're going to talk about might not be appropriate for them.

If the person who asks permission to join us is older than 19, then another kind of surprise happens sometimes when we vote no — although we almost never vote no. The reason we might vote no is if an adult wants to come to the meeting just to make sure that Alateen is going to be perfect for their child. Then we vote no, because it just feels too weird having some uptight parent in our meeting. Even if it means their kid can't or won't come to the meeting, it isn't good for us to have an adult like that, listening to us and judging what we're saying. Sometimes we just tell the adults that they can go to Al-Anon.

Our Alateen meeting meets at the same time and place as AA and Al-Anon, but we meet in different rooms. Most of us come with our parents, so that works out okay. But the problem is when our meeting ends.

Our meeting used to stop at the same time as the other meetings. Sometimes we had parents opening our door and telling kids that they had to leave right now or they wouldn't get a ride home. Sometimes they just opened the door so they could stand there and listen to us. It was pretty bad.

One night we made some changes. We still start at the same time as the other meetings, but now we close our meeting ten minutes earlier than before. So far, it's working out great. We get to talk to each other for a few minutes instead of racing out the door. And nobody bangs on the door and interrupts our meeting before we're finished.

Our group decided to hold open meetings once a month. The reason for our decision was that too many people were asking for permission to sit in on our regular meeting. Parents of new kids wanted to see what Alateen was like. A counselor wanted to see if Alateen would be appropriate for some of her students. Some college students wanted to use our meeting to help them decide whether or not to study to become counselors.

All of the people had good reasons for wanting to sit in on our meeting, but we were ending up taking care of them instead of taking care of ourselves. Sometimes we were avoiding talking about the things we really wanted to talk about. It felt creepy having strangers listening to us share our feelings. Since they weren't really Alateens, we didn't know if we could trust them.

Now when people come to the door and ask for permission to observe our meeting, we tell them to come on the third Wednesday of the month. We let the Al-Anon/Alateen information service know about our open meeting night so people can find out what to expect at our meeting when they call. So far, everything is working out all right.

Workshop On
TRADITION FOUR

Each group should be autonomous, except in matters affecting other Alateen and Al-Anon Family Groups or AA as a whole.

Complete the following sentences, adding as many sentences as you want.

To me autonomous means that each group ...

Our group can affect all of Alateen by ...

Our group can affect all of Al-Anon by ...

Our group can affect all of AA by ...

Group autonomy can be harmful when ...

TRADITION FIVE

Each Alateen Group has but one purpose: to help other teenagers of alcoholics. We do this by practicing the Twelve Steps of AA ourselves, and by encouraging and understanding the members of our immediate families.

In Alateen we have so many things that we can do to help ourselves. To help other teenagers of alcoholics all we have to do is share what we are doing for ourselves.

Talking about our problems is not the only reason for us to share at meetings. When we talk about our experiences with the Twelve Steps we are offering strength and hope to everyone who is with us in the room. The idea that just a little part of the Twelve Steps is working for us might be exactly what someone else needs to hear.

In our own families the same kind of thing can happen. Some little bit of encouragement we can give might attract someone we love into the wonderful world of recovery. And when things are not going well at home, there is always one more gift that we can offer our loved ones. We can look them in the eye, and with a quiet voice we can say, "I understand."

When I first came to Alateen I didn't believe what I heard. I didn't believe that so many kids were in the same boat that I was in.

Because I was so scared, I was absolutely convinced that everyone was lying. So I made up my mind that I would never come back. But when it came time for the next meeting, I decided to give it one more try. This time everybody said the same kinds of things they said the first time. The only difference was this time I believed them. In fact, I felt so comfortable that I didn't want to leave.

I've been coming to Alateen for about a year now. Every time I come I feel better than I did before. Alateen has helped me to live with, and love, the alcoholic in my life, again. It has taught me how to straighten out my life. If it wasn't for Alateen, I don't know what I'd be doing right now. I'm just glad I don't have to find out.

A long time ago my father promised that, no matter what, he would take me fishing. Well, everyone knows what happens when an active alcoholic promises something. That's right—it never happens. Well, my dad ended up not taking me, and he went out with his friends instead, drinking and playing pool. Not too long after that he hit his bottom, and he decided he needed help.

My dad found the help he needed, and he's been a recovering alcoholic for the past five years. He came up to me one day during his first year in sobriety. He said, "I want to make up to you for the promise I made about taking you fishing." I really didn't remember what he was talking about at the time. My disappointment had built up inside of me enough that I got it out at an Alateen meeting a long time before this.

My Alateen group was the warmest bunch of people I had ever met. I felt safe enough in their room that I cried my eyes out about a lot of stuff for a long time. And then the funniest thing happened. I turned into a happy person. I'd trust my Alateen friends with anything. They've always been there for me, and that's why I keep coming back.

It did feel good when my dad started considering my feelings, too.

My mother and I had never had a close relationship. I would always leave her out of all my problems. Alateen helped me to see that this was wrong.

Now I know how to ask my mother for her help, and she helps me get through my problems. I never thought this would ever be possible. I always thought my mother was my biggest problem.

Sometimes it takes listening to other Alateens for me to keep learning about myself.

My father was the alcoholic in my family. My mother got sick trying to make him stop drinking. She started going to Al-Anon where she found out that he was the one who had to have a desire to stop drinking alcohol.

After my parents got a divorce I used to see my dad every other weekend. I loved him a lot, and I liked going to see him. He had stopped drinking for a while, and then he started again. On a holiday in the middle of the summer my father decided to drink. He drank, and he had a heart attack at a party, and he died.

I felt so shocked and hurt. I loved my father, even though he caused lots of family crises and struggles in the past.

The help and comfort and support that I got from Alateen and Al-Anon is what saw me through those tough times. I used to worry about tomorrow. Now that I take it one day at a time, my life is smoother and much easier to deal with. No matter what I've had to talk about in my meetings, my friends in the program have always listened to me when I shared my feelings. It's their understanding and encouragement that's helped me grow.

✍

My dad came home from work one day all mad and stressed out. I asked him what was wrong, but he snapped at me. One of his friends called and asked him to go bowling. I didn't really mind when he went, but my sister had a funny look on her face. She knew my dad was going to go get drunk.

After my dad had been gone for a while I started to get worried. When I heard a car pull into our driveway, I thought maybe it was him. But it wasn't. It was my mom. A long time later my dad still wasn't home. Finally, my mom got sick and tired of waiting, so she told my sisters and me to start packing.

Just as we got outside my dad came home. When my dad asked my mom where we were going, she said, "To a hotel — until you get sober." Later that night I told my mom something I'd learned in Alateen — that we can't just run away from our problems. The next day we went home, and my mom and dad agreed to a separation. I still see my dad. All of us are trying to help my dad get through this.

I didn't get to know my real aunt and uncle until they stopped using alcohol and drugs. Now my whole family goes to AA or Al-Anon or Alateen.

I came to Alateen because my sister became so pleasant to be around after she started in Alateen. I think I'm gradually getting to be more pleasant to be around, too. The program is teaching me to share my feelings with others, instead of letting my feelings get all bottled up inside.

At first my mom didn't want me to go to Alateen. She was the Alateen sponsor, and she said that her group just couldn't get it together. Finally, they got some kids who were really looking for help. Then my mom started to let me go to the meetings.

Now I don't know how I could survive without it. It's my place where I can go and talk and not have to worry about someone judging me. And I know no one is going to repeat anything that I've said. It's a place where I can go and cry on someone's shoulder, if that's what I need. I know I won't be laughed at. It's even helped me improve the relationship I have with my favorite alcoholic. Plus, I have a lot more respect for my mom.

In my family, I am the second child of four. My father is a daily maintenance alcoholic. He comes home, drinks a large beer, and then he goes to sleep — that's my dad's master plan for staying away from my mother. My mother is the one who yells constantly and gives bad advice about everything I can think of.

What has hurt me the most about growing up in my family is their complete lack of interest in my life. Until I came to Alateen, nobody ever cared anything about me. The only thing I ever enjoyed before Alateen was sports.

I played basketball for one season. My father acted like all of the driving around he did for my practices and games was a big nuisance. When my parents were with me I felt embarrassed to talk with any of my friends. I felt like I had no right to talk. As a result of these experiences, I never went back to play any other sports, and I resented my parents for this for a long time. Even now my mother will always say that I had plenty of opportunities to play, but it was my decision not to. I still can't talk with her about it.

It was at my sister's "Parents' Day" for her volleyball team that I realized how Alateen has helped me to help my family. When it came time for my sister to introduce her parents, she said that they couldn't make it. She introduced me instead, as her sister — "who's kind of a real parent to me, anyway." Everyone clapped and welcomed me, and I felt so touched and surprised. Thanks to Alateen, I didn't feel alone in my family anymore. I'd finally heard someone in my family express a real feeling.

ALIVE

Today I know some boundaries — Yet I'm
happy, joyous, and free.
I thank dear God above — My Higher
Power, you see,
has given me a new way of life through
Alateen,
a program that's encouraging and guiding me.

Today I have a sponsor, a phone list, and
many friends.
I've been given the tools to turn my life
around.
Today I love myself for who I am and not for
what everyone would like me to be.
Today I have hope. Today I have a sense of
sanity.

Today I know that I'm not perfect, and that's
okay because I'm loved anyway.
Today I make mistakes and learn from them.
Today I can love and smile, and although it
may not seem very hot sometimes,
God's lit a fire that burns bright, deep down
inside of me.

I'll always remember my first experience at an Alateen meeting. The things I heard were really special. By the time someone asked me why I was there, I didn't feel uncomfortable at all. I felt like I could tell anything to everyone, even though there were people I knew in the meeting.

Alateen has helped me realize that I'm not the only one affected by alcoholism. Sometimes I feel like I don't belong in society yet, but Alateen is helping me to see that I do belong. I know that I'm not alone anymore.

✍

My family always equated love with money. No one ever said, "I love you." We gave each other gifts instead. In time, money grew real tight. From then on, everything came with a catch. I would be given something, only to be told that it had been bought with hard-earned money that we didn't have. The message I got was that I was a financial burden.

Needless to say, I felt very confused. I felt guilty and very angry with my parents for accusing me of being a burden. It wasn't my idea for them to give me gifts that we couldn't afford. But somehow it felt like they were blaming me.

I never learned the meaning of love until I joined Alateen. In Alateen I didn't have to give anything to anybody, except to share my story, if I wanted to. I was accepted with open arms.

For the first time in my life, it didn't matter about money. The only thing around our Alateen table was love — unconditional, unquestioned, and complete. My life has never been the same since my first Alateen meeting. Now, I feel like there's a place where I belong.

Workshop On
TRADITION FIVE

Each Alateen Group has but one purpose: to help other teenagers of alcoholics. We do this by practicing the Twelve Steps of AA ourselves, and by encouraging and understanding the members of our immediate families.

Complete the following sentences, adding as many sentences as you want.

The purpose of Alateen groups is to...

I encourage other members of my family by...

I understand my own family members when I...

When we stray from our purpose then we...

TRADITION SIX

Alateens, being part of Al-Anon Family Groups, ought never endorse, finance or lend our name to any outside enterprise, lest problems of money, property and prestige divert us from our primary spiritual aim. Although a separate entity, we should always cooperate with Alcoholics Anonymous.

Little by little, in a kind and gentle way, we learn how to mind our own business. We learn how to feel good about ourselves, and we learn to be grateful for all the help we have received from Al-Anon and from Alcoholics Anonymous.

Alateen is a simple program. We recover through the Twelve Steps. We stay united through the Twelve Traditions, and we serve each other through the Twelve Concepts.

From time to time, a lot of us find ourselves saying, "Let's Keep It Simple."

Alateens Share On
TRADITION SIX

To me the most important reason for not using the name Alateen on any outside activity is to protect our anonymity. It's nobody else's business if someone in our family is recovering from alcoholism.

When I tried joining other organizations and clubs I always wondered what they really wanted. Sometimes I found out that their real purpose was to make somebody else look good. You know, so they could brag about how many members they had or about how much money they had in their treasury.

Alateen is the only organization I've ever been a member of whose primary purpose is to help me feel better about myself and my family. All of my friends in the program know that it's not my mom's fault that she's an alcoholic. At the same time, nobody wants me to put up with my mom hurting me anymore, either. Alateen is helping me keep my mind and both of my eyes wide open.

I found out about Alateen because Alcoholics Anonymous told my dad about it and he told me. I think we should always cooperate with AA, because they cooperate with us.

It's nice to know that even though Al-Anon and Alateen are separate entities from Alcoholics Anonymous, we can still cooperate with AA in some very significant ways. For instance, one of the sponsors for our Alateen group is an AA member. He didn't have to volunteer to assist us when we needed help, but he did.

One of the ways that our group cooperates with AA is that we provide Alateen speakers for their functions. Since both

Al-Anon and Alateen came from the program of Alcoholics Anonymous, it's good that we can still help each other.

✍

We had to be careful in the way our group chose its name. We didn't want to give the impression that we were connected to a church, just because the church was nice enough to rent us a meeting room. So we named our group after the day of the week on which we meet and the community where the church is located. That way, newcomers will have an idea whether our meeting might be convenient for them. And we don't have to worry about leading them to believe something that isn't true.

✍

Tradition Six frees our group from making decisions on how to use our funds wisely. By not being allowed to finance outside projects, we learn to be financially independent and rely on our own funds to maintain our group needs. We buy literature for our group as well as for newcomers who attend our meetings.

Workshop On
TRADITION SIX

Alateens, being part of Al-Anon Family Groups, ought never endorse, finance or lend our name to any outside enterprise, lest problems of money, property and prestige divert us from our primary spiritual aim. Although a separate entity, we should always cooperate with Alcoholics Anonymous.

Complete the following sentences, adding as many sentences as you want.

To never lend our name to an outside enterprise means to ...

Our group would be endorsing an enterprise when ...

Our primary spiritual aim is to ...

Money could divert us from our primary spiritual aim by...

We can cooperate with AA by...

This Tradition can apply to my personal life by ...

TRADITION SEVEN

Every group ought to be fully self-supporting, declining outside contributions.

By paying our own bills, buying our own literature and getting our own refreshments, we become independent. Whether our group collects all of the money through donations from members, or if we raise the money by working on fund-raisers, the important thing is we took the responsibility to figure out how to do it.

Even the refreshments taste better when we practice the Seventh Tradition through our own actions.

Alateens share on
TRADITION SEVEN

Our group has had some difficulty with Tradition Seven. The main problem is our responsibility to pay rent for the room we use for our meetings When we get back on track with the rent, then we'll start to deal with our needs for literature. Eventually we might even be in a position to make contributions to the World Service Office. It's a slow process, but we're making some progress.

The Alateens in my home group don't have a lot of money. It makes a difference sometimes when we need to pay our rent or buy literature.

It's hard for us to be independent. AA and Al-Anon have offered to help us out, but we want to be on our own. Our sponsor made an arrangement with the people who own the building where we have our meeting. Each month we give a percentage of what we collected. So our rent is forty percent of what we collect. Since we always collect something, we can always pay our rent.

When I came into Alateen I was looking for answers to my problems. My mother and father were in the process of getting a divorce. I felt like I was trapped, living inside an emotional punching bag.

In Alateen I learned how to grow. I learned that I got what I gave. I had to make a contribution in order to get help. It wasn't a money contribution. It was me. I had to contribute a little bit of myself. That's what helped me grow. I found out that Alateen is a 50/50 program.

I remember all of the frustrating discussions I had with my parents when I was growing up. For as long as I can remember, I always wanted to be independent. But my parents always said as long as I was living under their roof I'd have to follow their rules. I used to just sit and dream about the day when I would finally be financially independent —

then I would be the one who called the shots.

That's why Tradition Seven is one of my favorite Traditions. Tradition Seven means to me that as long as we as a group are truly taking responsibility for our own expenses, then no one can come in and tell us what to do.

We are the decision-makers when we're paying our own way. And maintaining our financial independence means that we can keep the focus of our meetings on the primary purpose of our program—which is us. We can concentrate on how we can help ourselves and others like us who are affected by someone else's drinking. We don't have to surrender, even a little bit, to outside forces that want to pressure us into doing things their way. Tradition Seven keeps us in charge of ourselves.

The only way I've been able to get any money is by keeping my bus money and walking home. My dad doesn't have much money but he won't let me get a job. Sometimes I help a friend who has his own newspaper route, but if my dad found out about it he'd have a fit. I don't know why my dad is like that. I think he wants to keep me dependent on him for as long as he can.

Alateen tells me it's important to take care of myself, but it's hard when my dad doesn't want me to take care of myself. I like the meetings though. I wish I could donate some money to help pay our expenses, but I don't have any.

Sometimes it's easy to get away with not supporting my group. In my group when they pass the basket I can justify myself by saying, "Hey, I'm just a kid. I'm a student—you know I don't have any money."

Yeah, but what happens when I realize that I didn't have spare change for my group, but I had money for junk food or CDs and videos? Oh brother, I guess a quarter or even fifty cents won't hurt me once a week.

After all, it's my group. It's where I found my serenity, not to mention more of a family than I've ever known.

✍

Recently I attended a meeting where no Seventh Tradition donation was collected because no rent was being paid. I felt very uncomfortable there.

I give Seventh Tradition money to my meetings so I can have a say in what goes on. While not paying rent is a luxury, and sometimes a life-saver, I'm afraid the landlord will eventually start to make his wishes known. Somehow he'll let us know how he wants us to run our meetings. Then our focus will be lost.

For the money, I don't think it's worth it—to run the risk of losing what Alateen really means to a lot of us.

✍

Service is also part of the Seventh Tradition for me. I may not be able to give money all the time, but I can do a lot of other things that help my group. All I have to do is look around our meeting room. There's always something that I can do.

✍

Tradition Seven teaches us how much we can accomplish when we work together. By taking financial responsibility for ourselves we realize how important we are as individuals. Being self-supporting is also a way that helps us bond our group together.

In my Alateen family we always vote before we spend any money. No one decides for the rest of us. It's up to everyone to say what we think and how we feel, but no one takes action until everyone agrees.

At home my parents can't even agree with each other. One time my dad decided to buy a refrigerator. He didn't say anything about it to my mom. When the deliverymen came to the door mom wouldn't let them bring our new refrigerator inside the house. When my dad came home he found the refrigerator sitting outside on the front porch. Mom was mad at him for spending so much money without even asking her about it. Dad said he wanted it to be a surprise—so mom threw a coffee cup at him, and she cried in her bedroom for the rest of the day.

I like the way we do things in Alateen. I wish my family could make decisions the same way that my Alateen group does. I think everyone would like it better, even my dad.

We were shocked to find quite a bit of money was missing from our group's treasury, so we decided to make some changes. Now we always have two members count the money after every meeting. They write the amount and the date in our signup book. We also decided to open a bank account for our group. Two members have to sign at the same time to get any money out of our account. We're trying to be fully self-supporting by doing some things to protect ourselves.

✍

I didn't trust people before I came to Alateen. So when I saw they passed a basket at my first meeting, I thought that must be the catch. Even when the treasurer told me that I didn't have to put anything in the basket because it was my first meeting, I thought they'd catch up to me later on.

As it turned out at all of my meetings, not just at the first one, every time they passed the basket it was always voluntary. Everyone put in what they could, if they could. If they couldn't put in anything, then it was still no big deal.

I also remember when the treasurer explained to me that whatever was collected became the group's money. Wow—I thought she probably got to keep the money for herself. Maybe she got to go shopping with it—I mean, she really wore nice clothes. But if it became the group's money? I didn't know what to think about that. She must have guessed what I was thinking, because as soon as I thought it she said, "The group uses the money to pay rent for our meeting room. And we use it to buy literature and some cookies and maybe some hot chocolate.

Then I started noticing when the basket went around the room that some members put in change and some even put in a dollar or two. It was almost too much for me to handle when I realized where all of the stuff for our meeting really came from.

I'm really grateful for what so many members gave to our group. I'll even admit that for a few meetings, part of what really made me keep coming back was the hot chocolate.

I'm the group representative for my Alateen group. Many of our members wanted to go to our area convention in May and to an Alateen conference in August. Our main problem was that we didn't have enough money to pay for our expenses. We decided to raise money so that as many members as possible would have a chance to go.

We held bake sales at Al-Anon meetings. We helped organize an Alateen sponsor workshop where we sold refreshments. We had a dance and we invited members from Al-Anon, AA and other Alateen meetings to attend.

It was hard to get everything organized, but we did it. Our group raised enough money, and we learned a lot about ourselves and about each other in the process. I think everybody would agree that it was well worth our effort.

Part of what I learned from the Seventh Tradition in Alateen is that I also need to help out in my home. When I do my chores with the right attitude, I feel like my family belongs to me, too. It's not like I just belong to my family.

Our group developed a list of ways in which we could raise enough money to support our group.

One way is through weekly contributions at meetings. Members choose whether or not to contribute. We pass a basket at meetings with a globe on it. This money is used to send our group representative (GR) to assembly meetings and

Alateen conferences because we feel it is important for our group to be represented. It is also used to make contributions to the World Service Office. The money collected goes toward expenses such as literature, including a library of books, a donation for the use of the room in which we hold our meetings, refreshments and donations to the local information service.

Another way we raise money, is by having an annual open house meeting. A committee is formed so that we don't take time from meetings to organize the open house. The committee does things such as make up flyers to send to other meetings and seeing that everything is set up properly. We hold a raffle in which we offer prizes such as an Alateen or Al-Anon book or a plant. The money helps to support us throughout the year.

When we hold open house, we especially note the Seventh Tradition: "Every group ought to be fully self-supporting, declining outside contributions." An important part of our group is that everyone is involved. The responsibilities are shared so all the members are able to feel a part of the group.

We decided that we'd like to have refreshments during a ten-minute break in the middle of our Alateen meeting. Our sponsor volunteered to buy what we wanted, but he said he needed us to tell him what to get. When we told him we'd like a powdered fruit drink, he asked how much we thought it would cost and if we had the money to pay for it. After we finished all of our discussions about this we realized that it might take a few more meetings before we would have enough money to buy what we wanted.

Workshop On
TRADITION SEVEN

Every group ought to be fully self-supporting, declining outside contributions.

Complete the following sentences, adding as many sentences as you want.

I can support my group by ...

Outside contributions include ...

It is important to be self-supporting because ...

When our Alateen group is not self-supporting then we ...

The ways we can be self-supporting include ...

It is important to make regular group contributions to the district, area and World Service Office because ...

Some of the benefits from our district, area and World Service Office as a result of our donations are ...

I support <u>myself</u> physically, emotionally and spiritually by ...

TRADITION EIGHT

Alateen Twelfth Step work should remain forever nonprofessional, but our service centers may employ special workers.

Not everyone has experienced the kind of spiritual awakening that it takes to carry the message to teenagers who still suffer. The best ones to deliver that message are the ones who have lived it — us.

Special workers do a lot of the jobs that are necessary for our service centers to remain open, but they don't do the biggest job. When one Alateen talks with another teenager about experience, strength and hope, the message always comes from the heart.

Alateens share on
TRADITION EIGHT

It amazed me when I worked in the Al-Anon/Alateen office during school vacation. A lot of people called the office during the day. All of them wanted to talk with me.

I told them how they could go to a meeting. I looked at a big map on the wall so I could find meetings near their home or their school or their work. They thanked me, and sometimes they asked me for my name. Of course, I just gave them my first name.

When I've spoken at school assemblies the reason the audience listens to me is because I'm talking about alcoholism in my own family. I don't tell anybody what to do, but I share what happened in my home, what I did about it, and how everything turned out.

When I'm finished talking somebody always says, "How did you get the courage to tell everybody the truth about your life?" Nobody ever says, "I don't believe you."

The Al-Anon/Alateen service center in my town is an information service and a literature distribution center. We sell Conference Approved Literature (CAL) pamphlets, books, posters, and tapes. We print a monthly newsletter and a schedule of all the Al-Anon and Alateen meetings in our area. Almost everything we do is done by volunteers.

We only have one part-time, paid employee. She does all of the banking and the ordering and the mailing. She works three days every week. The reason she's so special is because she's also a member of Al-Anon. I've learned a lot from her about how to work in an office.

In Alateen we help each other grow, spiritually and emotionally. Our program is not about graduating or getting straight As, or about rising to the top in anything. We don't get paid for what we do in the program, unless you call getting a better life a kind of payment.

Service is what we do for ourselves and for other people.

Every time we share our experience, strength, and hope with someone else, we are helping ourselves. Every time we tell the truth about ourselves in a meeting, or try to figure out why we do some of the things we do, we are probably also helping someone else.

That's just the way it works in Alateen. We receive by giving, and we give by receiving. It's different and it works.

✍

There are lots of responsibilities and jobs that need to be done to keep Alateen in motion all around the world. One of the most exciting things for me to experience was when I visited the World Service Office for Al-Anon and Alateen.

I couldn't believe all of the things that special workers do every day to help keep our program alive. There is so much literature to write and edit and translate into all of the major languages in the world. There are so many books and pamphlets to ship everywhere. There are expenses to meet and donations to record.

I'm glad that everything gets done as well as it does, considering all of the difficulties in serving so many members and independent groups all over the globe. I'm glad that volunteers don't have to do everything.

✍

Our Alateen group was started by people who just wanted to help themselves. I think that's what makes our group so special. We try to share only what we've learned from each other. We talk from the heart. I think it's this heart-talk that brought us together, and I think it's the heart-talk that keeps us coming back.

Reach out and touch the Alateens !! !! !!

Our group has two sponsors. One is a long-time Al-Anon member. The other sponsor is a professional counselor who has been in Al-Anon for several years.

Both of our sponsors speak only from their Al-Anon experience when they share in our meeting. The sponsor who is a professional counselor says the reason why she comes to Alateen is because it is good for her.

I am the group representative of my Alateen group. I've been to a lot of area assemblies and district meetings. Each one has taught me more than the one before. It is very fulfilling to keep my meeting and Alateen running as smoothly as possible.

I used to feel like my opinions were worthless and nobody cared or listened. I expected the same when I first attended an area assembly meeting, so I was quiet and just listened. Finally, I got comfortable and realized that my ideas and opinions were important and useful. Now I actively participate in many service activities. Service work is a big part of what keeps me healthy in Alateen.

Workshop On
TRADITION EIGHT

Alateen Twelfth Step work should remain forever nonprofessional, but our service centers may employ special workers.

Complete the following sentences, adding as many sentences as you want.

Service centers include ...

Nonprofessional means ...

Service centers may or may not hire and pay special workers because ...

Twelfth Step work includes ...

I can do Twelfth Step work by ...

TRADITION NINE

Our groups, as such, ought never be organized; but we may create service boards or committees directly responsible to those they serve.

No one in Alateen is in a position of authority over another member. All of us are equals. We serve each other, but we do not govern each other. Alateen is one of the most democratic organizations in the world. Everyone's voice counts, but no one's voice counts more than anyone else's.

Alateens share on
TRADITION NINE

When I first started in Alateen I thought the group representative, treasurer and members of the steering committee were the people in charge. I thought they had all the power. I knew there was something different about them and I just assumed that it was power.

It wasn't until after I was elected treasurer that I realized what was really going on. The officers didn't have authority or power that made them so different. They just happened to be happy. Even after they stopped being officers, they were still happy.

I didn't understand Tradition Nine when it said our Alateen groups weren't "organized." After all, our group had structure — we had a chairperson, a secretary, a treasurer, two sponsors, speakers, topics, and we had even elected a group representative.

Then someone explained that we are all "trusted servants," doing service for our group and for Alateen as a whole. The key is that none of us who serve can govern or boss any of our group's members. No one is the dominant member. No one becomes the ruler of anyone else in the group.

Now I get it. Our group experiences have shown that it's best for us to be equals. That's why we form committees, so we can all work together. We can have a committee that works to put together the group's anniversary celebration. Or we can have one that works on public information to get the Alateen message to schools, churches, and youth groups. When we work together, then we can grow together.

At my third Alateen meeting the group secretary didn't show up. We just sat there looking at each other until one of the old-timers turned to me. She said, "Would you be willing to lead tonight's meeting?"

Now I'm not the kind of person who volunteers to do a lot of extra things, especially things that I've never done before. At home I don't volunteer to do anything, because if I do then somebody will steal my whole day away. But Alateen is different.

Actually, I felt flattered that she would ask me if I wanted to lead the meeting. I didn't think I'd been around long enough to be in charge of anything. Then it occurred to me that she might think I was somebody else, or maybe she thought I went to a lot of other meetings besides this one.

Finally, she said, "All you have to do is read what it says on the paper. If you need any help, just ask." I did it. I led the meeting. Afterwards, even the sponsor said I did a good job.

I hate it when someone says who's supposed to talk in a meeting. I don't think we should pick who talks. I think it's okay if we go around the room in a certain order, as long as people can pass if they want to. I think it's okay for someone to break the order too, if they really want to say something.

But the kind of meeting I like best is when anyone can volunteer to speak. All they have to do is introduce themselves by their first name and start talking.

I like it when the leader volunteers to lead the meeting on a certain Step or subject and then when she's done she says, "If anyone else would like to speak on this subject or on the subject of your choice, please feel free. Thanks for listening."

✍

For a long time our Alateen group ran without very much of a democratic process. Every week our sponsor would collect the money and give us the topic for our meeting. And whoever got the mail would read it. It got to the point where no one wanted to go to the meeting. Finally, the sponsor resigned.

With our new sponsor, we decided to elect officers who would be responsible for getting and reading the mail, collecting the money, and leading the meetings. We even have a group representative to represent us at the area assembly. By following Tradition Nine, we now have members who will guide and be responsible — without any one person controlling or dominating the meetings.

Workshop On
TRADITION NINE

Our groups, as such, ought never be organized; but we may create service boards or committees directly responsible to those they serve.

Complete the following sentences, adding as many sentences as you want.

Types of service boards might include ...

When we say our groups should never be organized, we mean ...

When our group has a workshop or dance, the committee is responsible to those they serve when they ...

"Those they serve" means ...

Our local committees on which I might serve are ...

TRADITION TEN

The Alateen Groups have no opinion on outside issues; hence our name ought never be drawn into public controversy.

In Alateen we share our experience, strength and hope in order to overcome the effects that someone else's drinking has had on our lives. We work the Twelve Steps adapted from Alcoholics Anonymous ourselves, for our own personal recovery. We follow the Twelve Traditions of Alateen in order to get along well with each other. We study the Twelve Concepts of Service in order to learn how to serve each other in a way that adds to our recovery.

Our sole purpose is to recover from the impacts of alcoholism. Anything else takes up precious time and might confuse people or give them a reason to stay away from the help that they really want. Whenever someone hears the name Alateen we want them to think about the full, rich, happy way of life that they can have if they just keep coming back and keep working the Alateen program.

Alateens share on
TRADITION TEN

When someone in our group brings outside issues into the meeting, one of the old-timers usually says, "We don't give advice to each other, or to the world."

My group used to have a lot of hurt feelings when we stopped talking about ourselves and started talking about what other people should do. It seemed like outside issues always hurt somebody's feelings first, and then somebody would get mad. When arguments lasted longer than our meeting did, then outsiders started hearing bad things about our group. It might even have kept new people away from Alateen. I hope not, but it sure helped us learn how important it is to keep our meeting a safe place for us to talk about ourselves, and not just about everybody else.

I'm glad that we don't let differences of opinion keep people away from Alateen. On every single issue there are probably people on both sides who have been affected by somebody else's drinking. Alateen is for all of them. And it's for all of us.

The way people perceive what our program is all about can carry a lot of weight. We have to be careful not to turn anyone away. If others see that we form cliques within the group, they might think it's the same in Alateen as it is in school, even though we know that it isn't.

Cliques also leave room for public controversy. For example, in our group if I start hanging around a certain clique and we talk a lot about a cause that's outside of Alateen, we might force the group to choose sides. Our unity would suffer. Some members might even think that the outside cause is somehow connected to Alateen, even when we don't intend to give anyone that impression.

Away from my Alateen meeting it's good to know that I can involve myself in any kind of cause or activity that I want, as long as I don't connect it to my Alateen membership. But it's also good to know that when I'm in an Alateen meeting I can concentrate on how alcoholism has affected me and my family, so I can learn how to feel better.

Alateen is special. I wouldn't want others like me, who are suffering in an alcoholic home, to be turned off about our program. I wouldn't want them to hear bad rumors or news reports about us. Let's keep it simple. Alateen is to help us recover from the impact of someone else's drinking. If we keep it that way, then all of us can get the help we need and want.

The whole country was talking about something that happened right in my home town. There were reporters from newspapers and television stations from all over the world. They came to take pictures and to interview people who might have some idea about what had happened to a girl from the high school that was next to mine.

One pretty smart newsman got the idea that the way this girl was treated probably had something to do with alcoholism. He showed up outside our meeting with bright lights and a camera crew. I guess he thought we'd be excited about getting our names and faces in the news.

Nobody would talk to him until he turned off all of his equipment. Then we told him that he could call the Al-Anon/Alateen information service office if he wanted to talk with someone. I don't know if he called or not.

I remember sitting in a meeting where a member started sharing about an event that had been on the news all day. Pretty soon other members started sharing about the same subject. Suddenly the entire focus of our meeting was on the news.

Fortunately, our sponsor jumped in and reminded us that Alateen is about us. She said that what goes on in the news isn't relevant during our meeting. She suggested that if we want to talk about the news we can wait until our break, or we can discuss it after the meeting.

All of us have had our lives affected by someone else's drinking. I've discovered that there is so little time to get the help I need in my weekly Alateen meeting that I just don't want our precious time spent on anything else.

Some of our group's members are involved with different school and church activities that focus on alcoholism. Even though some members are involved with these outside activities, which may have good intentions, Tradition Ten tells us that as a group, it is important not to support them because doing so would get in the way of our primary purpose. Alateen and Al-Anon are one and the same, despite the difference in our ages. We all share a common goal: a search for recovery.

Tradition Ten also shows us that every member of Al-Anon Family Groups, whether they be in Al-Anon or Alateen, have a place to belong.

Bringing outside issues into the Alateen meeting diverts us from our true aim. It makes members mad at each other and can create very sticky situations. Keeping the program out of public controversy protects our anonymity.

🖎

Growing up in my family, I always felt I had to defend myself and prove that I was right and good. I could not let it go when someone did not like me, especially if it was because they misinterpreted what I said or did. I had to convince everyone that I was a good person. I was probably trying to convince myself more than anyone else. What I did not understand is that I cannot please everyone and that it is okay if someone does not like me; it does not make me a bad person.

This personal sharing, I learned, relates to Tradition Ten. It says that Al-Anon and Alateen should not get involved in "outside" opinions or "public controversy." In the basic book of Alateen, *Alateen: Hope for Children of Alcoholics*, it states, "Even if someone should be speaking against us at the public level, we have found it is best to be silent and not get involved." Because of what I grew up believing, I did not understand this statement. Shouldn't we defend ourselves? What if someone thinks wrong of us? Can't we tell them the truth and make them believe we're okay?

What I learned after being in Alateen a while, and studying the Traditions in the groups I attended, is that I cannot control what others think about me or about Al-Anon or Alateen. I need to just work on myself. By doing this, I can show by example that I am a good person and that the program does work. Getting involved in a controversial issue, or trying to defend against slanderous articles or statements, would only draw negative attention to Al-Anon — attention it does not need. Actions speak louder than words, and if we all work our program and do the best we can do, those who know us will see how well the program really works.

Workshop On
TRADITION TEN

The Alateen Groups have no opinion on outside issues; hence our name ought never be drawn into public controversy.

Complete the following sentences, adding as many sentences as you want.

Outside issues are ...

Our Alateen group should not have an opinion on outside issues because ...

If Alateen allowed outside issues to be discussed then ...

An example of public controversy would be ...

Outside issues shift my focus because...

TRADITION ELEVEN

Our public relations policy is based on attraction rather than promotion; we need always maintain personal anonymity at the level of press, radio, TV and films. We need guard with special care the anonymity of all AA members.

No one wants to cause more trouble for the families and friends of recovering alcoholics. We have been through enough. We want to carry the message to those who still suffer, but we want to protect our loved ones from further embarrassment or pressure, too.

When we guard our anonymity, we do more than just protect our loved ones. We also tell newcomers that we will guard their anonymity too. We carry the Alateen message whenever we share our experience, strength and hope. Sometimes we do it by our actions, and sometimes we do it with words. No one is an "expert" on Alateen; we each express our own experiences in recovery.

Alateens share on
TRADITION ELEVEN

"Attraction rather than promotion" is one of the most difficult parts of practicing the Traditions for me. I feel like I've gained so much from working the Twelve Steps and the Twelve

Traditions that I want others to have the opportunity also. Inside, I jump around and shout, "Alateen is the way to go!" Outside, I quietly practice the slogans and hope that someone will see my example and ask me how I did it.

I know I don't have the right to preach Alateen to anyone. I also know that telling others my age what to do doesn't work. So I try to take such good care of myself that others will want to treat themselves the same way.

✍

My younger brothers caught the full impact of alcoholic behavior in my family. When I tried to help them understand what was happening to us, my dad made it extra hard on them. Eventually, the only thing I could do was to take care of myself.

Now I have a chance to help other kids. I speak whenever I get the chance. I tell the truth about what happened in my family. I listen while other people tell the truth about what's happening to them. I answer any questions that I know the answers to, and if I don't know the answers then I say I don't know.

Most importantly, I trust that my brothers have a Higher Power to help them too.

✍

My girlfriend came up to me one day and said, "What's going on with you? You seem to be feeling a lot better than you used to feel."

At first I thought she was just kidding around, but she wasn't. I told her that I'd been going to some Alateen meetings. I told her that my mother was an alcoholic and that my dad was living in a fog. She said she knew my mom had some kind of a problem and she knew that my dad was not in contact with reality.

So I asked her if that made a difference in how she felt about me. "Probably," she said, "because my dad's an alcoholic too."

Guess who started going to Alateen meetings with me?

✍️

A few members from our group wanted to have a car wash and donate the money to send our GR to assembly. Lots of members were willing to cooperate. We couldn't agree on what to put on our signs.

Some of us wanted to put the name of our group so we could attract more customers. Others wanted to put the name of our group on the signs just because we're proud of who we are.

After a lot of discussion we decided it wasn't right to break our anonymity by letting people know that we had relatives or friends who are alcoholics. So we decided to put on the sign — Car Wash/Donations. If people asked what the money was for we'd say it was for sending a kid on a trip.

✍️

I carried the Alateen message on television a couple of times. Boy, was that an experience — especially since I had my back to the camera, and my outline appeared in shadow. I turned my back to the camera because of our Tradition of anonymity. Whenever we carry the Alateen message of hope through any kind of media, whether it's TV, radio, or films, Tradition Eleven helps us put the focus on the principles of our program, instead of on our personalities.

Being in a studio can inflate one's ego. However, it is a very humbling experience to appear on television as a dark shadow, or to be identified on a radio program by your first name, only.

The principles of our recovery are far more important than being in the limelight of the media. After all, Alateen is about attraction, rather than promotion. By maintaining my anonymity, as well as that of the alcoholics in my life, I'm doing my part to help others feel safe enough to keep coming back.

When someone asked me to speak for Alateen at an Alcoholics Anonymous gratitude dinner, I told him I couldn't speak for Alateen. I could only speak for myself as a member of Alateen. He said, "Whatever, but you'll do it. Right?"

I agreed to go to the dinner, and I agreed to speak.

When we got there I couldn't believe how big the hall was. I couldn't believe how many tables were filled with people who were going to hear me talk. I felt so nervous that my lips started sticking to my teeth. My stomach wanted to climb into my throat. Even though there were piles of great looking food to eat, especially a whole line of tables filled with desserts, I couldn't eat more than just a little bit. I felt too sick to eat.

After dinner, the master of ceremonies introduced me as the first speaker of the night. He said my name, and he said I had come to speak for the Alateen program. Right away, I was able to understand why I was there and what I was supposed to do.

I looked out at the audience and I spoke straight into the microphone. I said my first name and I said I was a member of Alateen. I also said that I couldn't speak for the Alateen program — all I could do was to speak for myself. So I did. And when I finished I heard a lot of people clapping.

I felt so good that I started to eat.

✍

One of the things I've always loved about Alateen is the fact that you can take what you like and leave the rest. It's great how you can have your own opinions. In my home, I'm not allowed to have my own opinions or feelings.

I don't always agree with everything everyone has said in my meeting. That's why I'm glad we have Tradition Eleven. I can imagine what might happen if someone went on the radio and spoke as the representative of Alateen. What if they said something that I didn't believe in? The people who heard the radio might think that that person's opinions are exactly what Alateen is.

We all have our own experience, strength, and hope, and that's what makes us so special. Alateen has shown me that it's all right for me to have my own opinions and that other people can have theirs too.

✍

One of our long-time members was very popular. He shared his experience, strength and hope at other Al-Anon and Alateen groups, anniversaries and conventions. At school he was popular as well, and most people thought this guy had it altogether. Unfortunately, this young man stopped coming because of other obsessive behaviors. This taught our group how important anonymity is outside of Alateen. By remaining anonymous outside of the fellowship, this boy demonstrated that the Alateen program works even if our members don't work it or drop out.

Workshop On
TRADITION ELEVEN

Our public relations policy is based on attraction rather than promotion; we need always maintain personal anonymity at the level of press, radio, TV and films. We need guard with special care the anonymity of all AA members.

Complete the following sentences, adding as many sentences as you want.

The difference between attraction and promotion is ...

Personal anonymity means ...

Personal anonymity is important because ...

The difference between personal anonymity and personal anonymity at the level of press, radio, TV and films is ...

If one Alateen member talks to another on the Internet, they can stay anonymous by ...

I can go on TV and still be anonymous by ...

We can protect names and faces of people by...

TRADITION TWELVE

Anonymity is the spiritual foundation of all our Traditions, ever reminding us to place principles above personalities.

One of the big reasons why people feel attracted to Alateen is because we share our experience, strength and hope, anonymously.

Anonymity at Alateen meetings is like going to the mailbox and always finding valuable gifts for ourselves without knowing who sent them. It is like every day is our birthday.

In Alateen we keep getting presents from people we don't know, and we keep hearing a lot of encouragement to enjoy ourselves. It doesn't matter who sends the gifts or who gives the encouragement. It does not even matter if we say "thank you." What matters is that we take what we like and leave the rest.

Alateens share on
TRADITION TWELVE

When I first learned about my sister's alcoholism, I was shocked! I thought I must have been one of the most stupid people in the world not to have known that she had an alcohol problem. I went around saying there must have been signs, and it was my fault for not noticing. Other than being shocked, I was upset because I was afraid I had lost my sister forever. I thought she would change so much after treatment that the two of us could never be close again. My mom saw this in me and asked me if I wanted to try an Alateen meeting.

Alateen was something I had never heard of, so I had no idea what to expect. In the meetings it didn't take long for me to start to share my feelings. I talked, yelled, smiled, frowned, laughed, and cried. I learned in Alateen that I wasn't the only one who didn't know about a family member's alcoholism. I learned that maybe there weren't signs I could have noticed. I also learned that denial is something everyone experiences with this disease.

Most of all, I learned that Alateen is not only a place for me to share. It's also a place for me to listen to others share. Somehow, all of us help each other. I feel I've learned a lot about my sister and about myself by listening to other people talk about their loved ones. It's strange how someone we don't know can say exactly the right thing to help us with a very personal situation. I get the distinct impression, all the time, that through the program God is doing for us what we couldn't do for ourselves — and that no matter who we are, principles are more important than personalities.

✍

When I got the chance to go to an Al-Anon assembly, I didn't think much of the idea. I knew there were going to be a lot of elections. I knew people would argue about the candidates and the ideas, just like at school or in the government. The reason I decided to go was that I would have a weekend away from home. I also thought I might meet some Alateens from other cities.

The first night at assembly I got the impression that this experience might be a little bit different than what I'd expected. For one thing, they started the whole weekend with a get-acquainted session that was just like a big Alateen meeting. We talked about our feelings. Some of us talked about what we expected the assembly to be like, because it was our first one. Others talked about what was going on at home with their families and friends. I got to see what some of the adults in Al-Anon were like.

My biggest surprise came during the voting sessions on Saturday. A lot of people stood for office, and a lot of people spoke in favor of their own issues. The surprising part came after the votes were taken. Everybody hugged after the votes. People who stood for the same office hugged each other. People who voted against each other on different issues and ideas congratulated each other afterwards. I couldn't believe it. I couldn't believe how nice everyone was to everyone else. I am almost in a state of shock. And I'm really glad that I decided to go.

✍

Alateen is so anonymous that I always feel forgiven. When I make a mistake, nobody holds it against me. When I tell my group that I've made a mistake, they tell me to keep being honest.

I'm so used to people rubbing my nose in my mistakes that it feels weird when people keep being nice to me. Sometimes I wonder if they can see the real me. When I tell them that they say, "Keep comin' back. It works."

✍

I came to Alateen four years ago. Since then I've witnessed many progressive changes inside myself. By working the Steps and coming to meetings, I've been able to grow.

Recently, while talking with a friend, I discovered one way that I've changed. For the first time in my memory, I was not jealous of how pretty my friend is and how everyone liked her. I was not engulfed in self-pity. Instead, I appreciated our friendship, and I was happy that we could share as closely as we do.

Maybe this lifelong battle of trying to overcome envy has taken a turn for the better, thanks to Alateen.

I never knew how important the Traditions were until I wanted to help this really popular girl from my school find Alateen. When her alcoholic mom got drunk, she would hit the daughter. I was afraid to tell her about Alateen because I thought she would think that Alateen was just for less popular students like me. I thought it might be hard to convince her that Alateen is for all different types of people.

I finally told her about Alateen, and right away she asked me if any popular people went to the meeting. I made the mistake of telling her the name of someone she would recognize. She told her friends that my friend in Alateen has drunks for parents.

My friend from Alateen was very hurt, so much that she almost stopped coming to meetings. Of course, the girl I tried to save couldn't have cared less.

I forgot that even though it's important to carry the message, it's also important how I do it. I forgot to put principles above personalities. I forgot that I can tell people about myself, but who I see and what I hear at meetings, has to stay at the meeting.

In all my affairs today, from school to work to family and meetings, I remind myself, "principles above personalities." Today, I have a mind of my own and I don't need to be swayed by personalities or cliques. I only need to be swept away by the beautiful principles of my Alateen program.

I didn't trust anyone when I first started going to meetings. It took time for me to open up. Fortunately, my Alateen group practiced Tradition Twelve — "Anonymity is the spiritual foundation of all our Traditions, ever reminding us to place principles above personalities."

If my anonymity had been broken, I know that my dad would have left Alcoholics Anonymous. My mom would have left Al-Anon, and I would have left Alateen. Having outsiders know the truth about my family would have humiliated us. We wouldn't have been able to stick with our programs.

✍

I will always remember staring at the table card during my first few meetings. It said:

> Whom you see here,
> What you hear here,
> When you leave here,
> Let it stay here.

Wow! That's how I got comfortable when I first started coming to Alateen. Little by little, I started to share who I was and what was happening in my life. And gradually I started to let go of my pain.

I felt safe and protected because I knew anonymity was something I could count on in Alateen. At the same time, my sponsor always stressed that not everything should be spilled out at a meeting, because some of us have been more seriously affected by the disease than others have been. My sponsor suggested that the more intimate details of my life could be shared with a sponsor on a one-to-one basis. I'm so very grateful for all of the valuable help that I've been given through Alateen—more grateful than a lot of you will ever know.

✍

We all come to Alateen to learn to live comfortably in a home that has been affected by the disease of alcoholism. We carry many scars and hurts. Many of us have lost our ability to trust others. The Alateen program can help us trust again because we know that what we say at meetings will not be repeated. We can feel free to ask any questions without being made to feel dumb. We can talk about our hurt to others who understand. The most important thing about anonymity is that it protects us. By practicing anonymity, we help each other in a special way—by learning to trust others we also become trustworthy. By learning more about our Traditions, we grow as individuals, and our groups grow. When new teens come to us for help we are able to share with them our serenity, courage and wisdom.

☛

To me, anonymity is the spiritual foundation of my program. It's nice to go to a meeting and be known just by my first name. It doesn't matter where I come from, or what I have done because in Alateen I'm just me. No strings attached. I know how important it is to keep a person's anonymity. Some of us might get beaten by our parents, who are still drinking, if they knew we were going to Alateen. Anonymity is more than a courtesy; it is essential for our well-being and peace in the program.

☛

The first Alateen meeting I attended regularly was a Step and Tradition study group. I enjoyed reading from the literature and learning about the Steps, but I was not so willing to hear about the Traditions. My attitude was, "Traditions are boring. Why do we have to study them?" Fortunately, I kept an open mind and learned the importance of studying the Alateen Traditions.

Of the Twelve Traditions, the one I love to hear the most is Tradition Twelve. Growing up, I always looked at people's personalities. If I didn't like someone or thought them to be inferior, I hardly listened to what he/she said, including my mom. As a result, I was often surprised at what they had to say...especially my mom!

In order to fully understand how to "place principles above personalities," I first had to change my attitude toward those "inferior" people. I needed to remember that I do not know everything and that I can learn from anyone. I needed to get my pride and ego out of the way and open my ears and my mind to what others were telling me, regardless of their personality.

It says in Alateen's basic book, *Alateen: Hope for Children of Alcoholics*, "...We are all equals. (Tradition Twelve) teaches us humility. It's not who says it, but what is said that counts" (p.47). By others' modeling this behavior in meetings, I saw how this Tradition worked and was then able to practice it in my own life. I no longer think of my mother as just the alcoholic. I think of her as a human being and know that she can give good advice. Also, when I am at a meeting or at a service function, I remind myself of this Tradition and try to focus on what the person is saying rather than who is saying it. This makes listening so much easier, and I learn more too!

Workshop On
TRADITION TWELVE

Anonymity is the spiritual foundation of all our Traditions, ever reminding us to place principles above personalities.

Complete the following sentences, adding as many sentences as you want.

Anonymity is ...

Anonymity is spiritual because ...

Principles are more important than personalities because ....

An example of placing principles above personalities would be ...

When I place principles above personalities, I feel ...

SPONSORSHIP

Those Al-Anon members who have not been an Alateen sponsor for at least one meeting have no idea what THEY are missing.

Alateens and sponsors share on
SPONSORSHIP

My heart is full, and I have all the courage I need. Besides, I know where I can keep getting more courage every week. I get it from all of the young people I meet in Alateen. It takes a lot of courage to be a young person in an alcoholic home. Fortunately, these young people in Alateen have so much courage that they share theirs with me.

They don't even have to say anything. I can see the courage in their eyes when they come through the door. And when they finally decide to speak about their experiences, I hear my Higher Power giving all of us tremendous strength and incredible hope. I will always be grateful for the help that Alateen has given to me.

When I was ten years old my father told me he had a drinking problem. He said he was going to a far-away place for alcoholism treatment and then he was going to go to Alcoholics Anonymous.

My mother told me that my father would get help there. She also said that she was going to a place called Al-Anon. Then she said that I had to go to Alateen to get help for myself. I remember that all of these ideas seemed very scary to me when I was ten.

My mother and I went to see my dad. He seemed strange and different, kind of funny. I wasn't used to seeing him like that. He didn't even sound like my dad. He didn't smell bad anymore, either. Mom cried a lot, and nobody told me anything.

Mom forced me to go to Alateen. I didn't like it. All of the kids were bigger than I was. I didn't feel like talking to anybody, but I kept coming back, even after my mother stopped making me go. All of that was over ten years ago.

I continued in Alateen, and then I went into Al-Anon. Now I help sponsor an Alateen meeting. I'm really grateful to my mother for making me go to Alateen until I wanted to go. The strength and courage I have gained through the program have changed my life. I live a lot differently today than the way I lived before.

✍️

How can I even begin to explain the miracle of sponsorship in my life? The first lesson I received was that surrender isn't about weakness, it's about strength. My sponsor practically took my hand and showed me how to trust her. She told me even if I felt scared and suspicious to "act as if" I trusted her and it would come. I found that by asking for help from my group, my sponsor and eventually my God, I had a different sort of strength, one I never knew existed. That strength to me is freedom.

✍️

When I got to Alateen, I had no self-worth and I did everything to push people away from me. I was so afraid of being hurt one more time. I grew up with the confusion of alcoholism, loving and hating my alcoholic mom and not understanding the violence and constant yelling in my house. I quickly picked up the weapons to hurt the people I loved the way I was hurting. My biggest fear when I got to Alateen was that I would turn out exactly like my mom. Alateen gave me hope for the first time. I knew and felt that I was not alone.

What has sponsorship done for me? I could hardly imagine my recovery without a sponsor. My sponsor has loved me, supported me, guided me and encouraged every ounce of enthusiasm I have for this program. The hardest part for me in asking someone to sponsor me was trust. By the time I got to Alateen I trusted no one and had so many secrets I planned to take to my grave. My sponsor started spending time with me and sharing her story with me. I thought, "If she can tell me this stuff I can tell her about my life." I had to come to the point that I was willing to accept help and use the guidance being offered to me.

When I began my transition from Alateen to Al-Anon, that is when I really started working with a sponsor. For the first time, I worked the Steps with her honestly. I came to a painful time in my recovery where it was time for me to start growing or I would never stop the insanity in my life. I learned how to trust my sponsor and in learning how to trust her I began to trust others. I am learning how to communicate with her and follow direction. I asked her for help and in doing that, I admitted powerlessness.

Personal sponsorship with girls in Alateen is a privilege. The neatest experience I went through was seeing that all that pain in my past counts for something because I get to share it with someone else and help them through their pain. When I was new, people gave me so much hope just being honest with me about their own lives. I am grateful in turn today that I can give someone that kind of hope, too. I really see how God works in their lives which reminds me of how God works in my life. Most of the time I feel like the girls I sponsor help me far more than I help them.

More than anything, I treasure Alateen and what it has given to me—a life with a purpose. My sponsor plays an important role in my life helping me to work with newcomers and sharing her experience with me. I follow the direction she gives me and when I am faced with a problem beyond my experience I ask for help.

Another gift in sponsorship is with service because my sponsor encouraged me to raise my hand for commitments. My sponsor and other Alateens walked me through these service commitments and now I get to do that also. There is nothing more exciting than to watch the lights come on in someone else. Working with others, you watch them change and grow through the Twelve Steps and service commitments. I love to watch newcomers find solutions to their problems.

That is the most exciting part of helping others, to see the hope and the joy happen in someone's life. I am responsible for carrying the message and passing it on exactly how I received it. I am so grateful that God works through people because most of the time I am telling one of the girls I sponsor exactly what I need to hear myself. I am in debt to Alateen and I am willing to go the distance to help someone else find hope. I am excited about life, Al-Anon and Alateen and try to carry the message in whatever way I can. I am so grateful Alateen carried the message to me and that I did not leave before the miracle happened in my life.

When I first came to Alateen, I was scared, but I shared and I felt better. I started to go all the time. Working the program was not easy at first. So, I got a personal sponsor, but she lived so far away. I couldn't see her much. Then, I got a new sponsor and I really liked her. I got to see her a lot when I needed someone to talk to. She was always there. After a few months, someone asked me to sponsor them. I was honored, so I did. We would talk, but after a while she stopped coming to the meeting and I never saw her again. I did my First Step. I felt so good. After a while I stopped calling my sponsor. I wasn't feeling good, but my sponsor called me. After two years, I feel great. I did my Second Step and I love my sponsor. I'm so grateful for my program!

Before Alateen I really didn't have any kind of excitement for life. I always thought I was going to grow up to be a nobody and do nothing with myself. I didn't think I was worth feeling good.

When I walked into the room of Alateen, people made me feel welcomed and loved. Everyone asked if I had gotten a sponsor yet. I had not, but it seemed important so I asked one of the girls who had been calling me. From the very start my sponsor always loved me unconditionally, even when I wasn't doing the things she had suggested. No matter what I did, my sponsor never threw me away. Now by working the Steps with my sponsor, and following her direction I have a program today, and I have a love for life.

Today I get the gift of sponsoring people. Sponsoring other people has taught me how to love others unconditionally. I get to be a friend who gives love, and in return receives love. I get to pass the program on just the way I got it when I was new. That way it does not become diluted. By working the Steps with others I get to go through the Steps again and each time I learn more about myself. Because of the Steps, today I have a responsibility to my God and to this program to carry the message of Alateen.

When I get down on myself and start thinking that I am a nobody I get to remember that God has freely given me this program and in order for me to keep it I must give it away. That makes me feel really good and I get excited because I know I have a purpose today. My purpose is the Twelfth Step, "... to carry this message to others, and to practice these principles in all my affairs."

After experiencing some of the early joy of recovery, complacency began to develop in my recovery. For a long time, my recovery energies were concentrated on issues concerning self-worth. At the time, I did not know that worth was something I already had. Alcoholism progressed in our family and finally our family separated. The separation presented me with a different set of needs and the loneliness encouraged me into action. The answer was simple: Alateen sponsorship.

The fellowship of Alateen taught me of the joy of childhood. Just as the sky is defined as the playground for birds,

Alateen is the playground for young adults. Playgrounds are traditionally safe, well-protected areas where young people gather to exchange ideas and experiment with growing up. Alateen provides this "playground" for young adults and their sponsors to grow under the supervision of a nonjudgmental adult rather than being isolated and exposed to the wrath of family members or peers.

Listening and supporting the efforts of our younger members prepared me for a new challenge: letting go of my three children. Not to be confused with abandoning, letting go hurts. Alateen sponsors understand, as few others can, the unspoken horror of alcoholism. Through this bonding of spirit, the other side of responsibility begins to surface. Not only do we have a responsibility to ourselves, we also have a responsibility to others. Alateen sponsorship works, for this I will remain forever grateful.

✍

By the time I reached Alateen, I was a fourteen-year-old girl hardened by the effects of alcoholism in my home. I was locked up inside because I was full of anger, keeping secrets, wearing a facade and refusing help from anyone.

I was always angry. My father received so much ridicule, criticism and antagonism from me, I remember screaming at him so loud I thought my head would explode. I thought that because I could stand up to my father that made me strong. In Alateen I learned everyone was hurting as deeply as I was, but without a program I just couldn't see past myself. I felt so sorry for myself. My mother once said to me, "Why is it that everything you see is black?" I knew what she meant, hardly a day passed in which my anger and self-pity didn't consume every area of my life. There was nothing, in my opinion, to be happy about. I felt cheated by my parents, by the world and even God. With all these intense feelings, I found each day harder and harder to maintain my strong image.

I wanted so badly to not be affected by my father's drinking and everything that went with it; losing jobs, cars, houses, moving from state to state, living homeless in a campground and with other people, changing schools and having to make new friends and come up with new lies to cover up, waiting for rides and getting picked up late or not at all, trying to hide the money problems and pretending we weren't really poor when we were on welfare, wearing second-hand clothes, eating donated groceries from the church, and riding the county bus. No matter how hard I tried to avoid it, my dad's drinking had affected my personality and my life. Today I understand that's what makes it a family disease and I'm not unique in any of my feelings or experiences. It's just what happens in an alcoholic home.

I have continued to hear, since I came to Alateen, how lucky I am for receiving recovery so young. I always say back, "We all get here right on time, exactly when we're supposed to which is God's timing." For one of the first things I heard my sponsor say was that eventually you end up where you're headed and I was bent on self-destruction. Alateen saved my life and no one can argue otherwise to me. I was not quite beyond reach when Alateen got hold of me. I had a tiny spark of hope left and they fanned that flame into the enthusiasm I have today. They saw right through my facade and seemed to know me better than I knew myself. They put names to my crazy feelings and kept saying over and over that I was not alone anymore. I was free to be the real me, but I didn't know who the heck that was! That's where sponsorship came in.

In the beginning the whole group was my sponsor, then after I learned to trust Alateen as a whole, I realized the only way I could continue to grow was to get a personal sponsor. There was a lot of encouragement to do so in the meetings. It was positive peer pressure; everyone shared about sponsorship and I didn't want to be left out. The Alateens promised me I would find "me" once I was honest, open and willing enough to let someone really know me and love me unconditionally. It was awkward and scary at first. After all, I had been lying and covering up my true feelings for so long, I didn't know where to begin being honest and open with someone else. But I was willing and that's why it worked. It follows what I hear in meetings a lot, "If you don't take a chance, you don't have a chance."

My sponsor drilled into me the value of gratitude and that I didn't have to continue seeing the world black as my mom told me when I was a little girl. I remember once my sponsor asked me to try writing ten things I was grateful for before going to bed each night for thirty days. What I thought to be some sort of punishment turned out to be one of my greatest habits. I went past thirty days and although I don't make actual gratitude lists every night anymore, I do them whenever I feel self-pity or envy creeping up. Also, I've learned to get on my knees each night and thank my Higher Power for my past, for my present and for my future.

I continue on this journey not alone, but with a sponsor by my side. I believe that God speaks through people and my sponsor is simply the station I requested my Higher Power to come through on. Funny thing is there are girls in my life who call me sponsor. I just pass on what I've learned. It's awesome how this program has taken the experiences that caused me such devastating pain and shown me how to share them with someone else so we both get better! What I used to cry about alone, I can laugh about in sponsorship. My past can never hurt me again especially when I am using my experience to help someone else.

I believe that with one hand holding someone ahead of me (my sponsor) and one hand holding someone newer than me (someone I sponsor) I am a part of the link of recovery. I love sponsorship and I love my life. I am living happy, joyous and free — and the world is full of color!

Sponsorship was like the key to the locked cage alcoholism put me in. My sponsor was the first person I trusted, I respected, and I followed suggestions from. I gained willingness, through the trust I had for her, to venture deeper into the program working the Steps, taking commitments, going to their meetings, and eventually even making the transition into Al-Anon. To me sponsorship is about "Together We Can Make It" since I have learned that when I try to live my life alone the person I am hurting the most is me. I always encourage newcomers to not cheat themselves from the greatest gift to oneself which is asking someone to be a sponsor. If I were to go hiking up a very steep hill, which loving an alcoholic is to me, I would make sure I had a guide. And I would definitely want someone who has climbed it before and who believes I can climb it too. My sponsor took me through all Twelve Steps just as her sponsor did with her. It was terrifying and extremely painful at times, but my sponsor kept encouraging me to grow. I would look into her eyes and see her faith and somehow just believing that she believed in me made it okay to keep going. I hear in meetings all the time how people just wanted the serenity their sponsor had and I always laugh. Because I was so nervous, all I remember thinking was, "Maybe someday I'll be able to sit still in a meeting like she does."

Workshop On
SPONSORSHIP

**Complete the following sentences, adding as many
sentences as you want.**

The adult sponsor of my Alateen group provides ...

An Alateen group sponsor is ...

A personal sponsor is ...

I can use an adult sponsor to help me ...

I can use a personal sponsor to help me ...

To be a sponsor, I need to ...

WORKING TOWARD SOLUTIONS

Alcoholism causes many problems not only for the drinker but also for everyone else who is in contact with him or her. Sometimes it's on a daily basis. Other times contact is limited to weekend visits, vacations, etc. Using the Alateen program to cope can make a real difference in our lives.

Alateens share on
WORKING TOWARD SOLUTIONS

I'm really shy. At school it's hard for me to open up and talk to new people. If I don't know them, then I tell myself that I don't like them. I think of them as horrible monsters. That way, I never have to say anything to them. The thing is, I don't get to know more people this way. If I keep it up, I'll run out of friends.

In Alateen I'm trying to learn how to face my fears. I used to think courage was what people had when they didn't feel any fear. Now I see courage is what we can use when we do have fear.

✍

When I was little, about five years old, my mom would go in my room and go into this little he-man piggy bank. She'd steal all the money I had saved for so long. Then she'd use the money to buy booze.

When I was about ten years old, my mom would bribe me into giving her my money. If that didn't work, she'd just take it. Pretty soon she even bribed me to start drinking and taking drugs with her. When that happened it hurt me real bad to know that she would do something like that to me.

In Alateen I've learned to "Let Go and Let God." My sponsors and the other members have shown me that my mother truly is a sick person who's suffering from a disease. I have learned that under normal circumstances, none of those bad things would have happened to me or my mom. There are all kinds of prayers and little slogans that make everything so much easier. All I have to do is use them.

☜

I used to get so angry all the time. It just made me feel like a crazy person. I'd want to grab somebody and squeeze the life right out of them.

Then somebody in one of my Alateen meetings suggested that we try safe ways to express our anger. But I didn't even know there were any safe ways to be angry.

He suggested that when I got real mad at somebody I could try writing their name on the bottom of my shoe. Then, he said, I could spend the whole day walking on them.

It works.

Another thing he said to try is writing the person's name on a piece of paper. Then I could tear the piece of paper into tiny pieces, and I could flush it down the toilet. You know, by the time I watched the paper swirling down the drain, I started laughing.

The experience that has hurt me the most is when my uncle died. I didn't get a chance to say good-bye to him. This really hurt me deeply. Alateen helped me to express my anger about not being able to say good-bye.

If something goes wrong at school or at home and I want to scream, yell, or hit something or somebody, I always think of the Serenity Prayer. I say it over and over in my head and it calms me down. You'd better believe — I say it at least ten times every week!

I was a very lonely child. My parents were so wrapped up in their drinking that I felt like I was completely forgotten. When I became a teenager I continued to feel the same way, like I was always left out of whatever was going on.

After I joined Alateen my feelings changed. I started to feel like I was a part of something. I wasn't alone anymore. I felt like I was actually part of something good and healthy.

In Alateen I didn't have to make trouble to be noticed or to be accepted. Now if anyone doesn't accept me, I don't have to worry. There are plenty of people who do accept me. And I accept myself. If someone wants to leave me out of their life, then that's not my problem.

My stepfather is a dry alcoholic. He isn't drinking but he doesn't really know how to deal with things without alcohol. He tends to take out his feelings on the rest of our family.

With Alateen I've learned that my stepfather is hurting too, so if I can talk things out with him then we have a good chance to solve our problems without fighting. Alateen has helped me learn how to let go of my anger. I try to keep talking about what's bothering me. That way, things don't build up inside.

Committing suicide, I thought, was my only way out. I felt so alone and depressed because my family was caught up in alcoholism and drugs and organized crime.

I had all of the new toys and clothes that any kid could want. What I didn't have was the love of my parents. My mother hated children, so I grew up with nannies and security people instead of a family. I didn't even have friends, because we kept moving all the time. The police were looking for us constantly, so running away was all we could do. Even when they caught my dad and he went to prison, nothing changed. When he got out he went right back to the same stuff again.

I didn't know what to do. I made a lot of mistakes. I did not do well in school. I started drinking and doing drugs. Then I started thinking about suicide — you know, as a way out. Finally, I ran away. At least I got to spend more time with my friends.

Two of my friends told me about Alateen. My first reaction was the Alateens sounded like they must be a pretty sick group. I wondered how much was really wrong with them. Serenity sounded like a complete waste of time.

My friends got me to try Alateen. It shocked me to hear all of these guys talking about their families. I wasn't used to hearing anybody tell the truth about what went on in their home. Then it hit me. These people were helping each other. At the same time, I realized that I couldn't keep dealing with everything in my life all by myself. So I kept going back to more meetings.

When I told my mom about going to Alateen she really got mad. She and my dad were afraid that I was telling family secrets—which I was, but they didn't know that nobody was going to tell anything to anybody outside of the meeting. Sometimes when I came home from a meeting my mom would make up something so she could hit me or ground me. But after six months in the program even my mother could tell that it was doing me a lot of good. My father refused to see it, though. He resented both me and my mom. We were like objects to my father. I wasn't like a daughter. He loved money, not us.

I don't know what made my dad change. He still does a lot of bad things, but lately he's been helping me get to my meetings. Believe me, if Alateen can help me and my family, it can help anybody. Thanks. I love all of you.

✍🏻

Last year I lost a very close friend to alcohol. Because he chose to drive while he was drunk, two people died. He took his own life along with the life of a person who had chosen to ride with him.

I have a lot of friends who drink every weekend. I know I can't be there for them all the time. I can't make sure they don't drive drunk. The friend that I lost proved this to me.

In Alateen I've learned that I don't need to feel guilty. Instead, I've started giving my friends a choice. I can give them an alternative to going out and getting drunk. That way, if my friends go drinking and get hurt, it'll be their own choice.

✍

I'm very new to this program. Already I'm learning that talking about my problems really helps me find solutions.

I came here mainly because my father is an alcoholic. Even though my parents are divorced, my dad's problem really upsets me. He isn't the same person when he drinks. I don't get to see him very much, so it seems like such a waste for his drinking to spoil what little time we get to spend with each other.

Thanks to Alateen, now I have people that I can talk to about my problems. But I still have more problems to deal with. Like my dad getting remarried. I like his wife a lot. But sometimes I wish that my parents were still together. That way, I'd get to see my dad a lot more. But then, I'd miss his wife too. So, actually I don't know what to do. I don't know if I should be mad. I don't know if I should cry, or if I should hope. I'm sure Alateen will help me get through all of this, though, no matter what.

✍

The thing that pained me the most in my life was never meeting my father. We never talked about him, and when I did ask questions I never got straight answers. To this day it is a very sensitive subject for me that easily brings tears.

When I was five years old my mom and I lived with her boyfriend. I called him Daddy, because even at that age I knew he was the closest thing I'd ever have to a real dad. One day my mom and I were sitting on the bleachers watching a baseball game when I asked for the first time in my life, "Where is my real Daddy?" My mother said, "Right out there," and pointed to the baseball field. Just as she did, the game ended and all the players walked off the field. With everyone wearing the same uniform, I couldn't tell one player from another.

That night, when I got home, I made a promise to myself to meet my father. Someday when I was eighteen or nineteen I'd go to his home and he'd instantly recognize me and welcome me into his home. He'd be old and wise. At first there'd be tension — but more than a genetic bond, there'd be an emotional bond too. And I'd meet his wife and children, and there'd be love and friendship, instantly.

Well, that wasn't the way it turned out. During my junior year in high school we were given an assignment to write a play. Mine was going to be about what might happen if I did meet my father. When I shared this idea with friends they asked me questions. I answered them to the best of my ability. I said if my father rejected me again I'd seriously kill myself — and I'd make sure I wouldn't survive, because I didn't want to endure the pain.

I finally got my father's address. It was in a town I'd lived in only four years before. It was the same town where my grandmother and aunt still live. It turned out that I had gone to school with two of my father's children. I went to church with his wife and kids. I'd shopped at his uncle's and aunt's store, only half a mile from where I used to live with my grandma.

When I told my sponsor about writing to my father, she

asked me how I would handle the way he had rejected me. I was honest with her, and she said I might want to practice writing to him so the anger wouldn't show.

As I wrote letter after letter and began to let out some of my anger, I began to realize a few things about myself. The main thing that I realized is that I have survived seventeen years without my father's love and affection and attention. So I know I can live seventeen more without getting anything else from him. While I still mourn the loss of my father, I have been able to let go of some of my anger and give him some of my love. I can't explain how I can love a man I've never met, and it's not because he gave me life. I guess I just love him because he's there to love, and he probably needs it.

I did write to my father, and he didn't write back. That was over a year ago. In letting go, God gave me a gift. That's the gift of acceptance. I can't change or control my father, but I can move on. While half of my biological family is missing from my life, I have gained a wealth of family in Alateen and Al-Anon from all over the world. They can give me a gift my father can't — growth and serenity.

✍

I have some problems to discuss—my parents' drinking, my parents' separation, my parents and brother fighting, friends trying to commit suicide, my mother keeping me in the house all the time.

Alateens have helped me prove to myself that I can change my ways if I put my mind to it and then work on it. But it only works if I really want it to.

✍

287

The first time my mom mentioned Alateen I just ignored her. When she continued to ask me, I put off doing anything about it. Finally I ran out of excuses, so she took me to a meeting. I came into the meeting, sat by the door, and kept my mouth shut the whole time. I felt scared and out of place. I felt like I didn't have a problem with an alcoholic; his problems were a lot greater than mine anyway. So I felt like I didn't have a right to be there.

Well, I was wrong. I found out that I did have a problem. While I wasn't having a problem with my father, Alateen helped me realize that I was having a problem with my mom. The way she was dealing with the alcoholic was driving me nuts. The Alateen program helped me realize that I wasn't alone. A lot of us have more problems with our non-drinking parent than we do with the alcoholic.

The Steps, the Traditions, and the love and understanding in the program helped me to get where I am today. But first I had to realize that I wasn't the only one in the world who had this problem.

✍

Ever since I was very young, my dad has been a drunk. My oldest brother also became an alcoholic with little kids of his own. I always thought it was my responsibility to stop my dad and my brother from drinking. Alateen has taught me that it isn't my responsibility, so I feel better about that.

The problem now is my dad. I don't know how it happened, but one day at work he got his hand caught in a machine. He had to have surgery, but something went wrong during the operation. An infection started a disease in his whole body. Now he's paralyzed. Half of his body will be paralyzed for the rest of his life. This really scares me a lot.

Thanks for letting me share. It really helps me to say what I'm feeling.

I'm nineteen years old and a single mother of twin boys who are three years old. Their father left me when I was two and a half months pregnant. I was fifteen and pregnant when I moved here with my family. I didn't know anyone except my doctors and nurses. I guess it was about a year later that I was introduced to Alateen.

In the beginning I thought it would be a neat idea to go to the meetings. I knew I had all kinds of alcoholics in my family, and most of my friends were alcoholics too. I was pretty much surrounded by them. However, I never knew that I had a problem, personally.

I blamed everyone for everything and anything. I was good-looking and an excellent athlete, but I wasn't too good at anything else. So I tried to get what I wanted with my appearance and my sports abilities, and about 90% of the time I got whatever I thought I wanted.

My life is a lot different now. Alateen has taught me so much that it's wild. I admit that for the first three or four months in Alateen I just went for the love and the support. I could always count on that. I still didn't think I had a problem, but I always tried to fix everyone else's problems.

Finally I went downhill so fast that I needed to talk with someone. I felt so angry inside, so hurt. And I just couldn't stand my mother anymore. I had to do something. I called a friend who is in Al-Anon, and he asked me if I needed help. Of course I needed help right away, but it took a while for me to answer him. I did say yes, and he told me about love and detachment. It's really weird to know that I can love someone and still not like the things that that person says and does.

People always told me that if I wanted to learn more about myself and about how to help myself then I had to do some work. One of the things I needed to do was read. I hate reading, but I found some books in the program that I think are the best books in the world.

My first two and a half years in the program I did Steps One and Two. Then I hit bottom after staying away from meetings for a few months. When I came back to meetings it was like God was leading me by the hand. I did Step Three about a month later. I finished Step Three and started Step Four. It took me about three months to finish Step Four. Part way through Step Four I discovered some things about myself that were really hard for me to handle. The worst things that I discovered about myself were my experiences of sexual assault. The last time was during my job about three weeks before. It wasn't my first, but hopefully it's the last.

I'm learning about who I am, but I still have a long way to go. I'm learning about how the disease of alcoholism has affected me and about how it has made me sick. I'm not as sick as I was yesterday, and I'm not nearly as sick as I was three years ago. That's a really neat feeling.

I have a Higher Power — God. I trust Him, and I love Him. I love myself now. The program has given me so much. I really have a lot to be grateful for. I've found that great inner feeling when I'm so happy that words can't describe it, so I won't even try. I've found if I love myself enough I can deal with any problems with any of the alcoholics in my life. I just bless myself and go find a meeting.

✍

Loneliness is the very first feeling I remember. Since I was a real little kid, that lonely feeling has always been inside of me. I've also felt awkward and stupid, especially in a crowd. When other people were around I almost always felt drop-dead miserable. I built shields and guards around myself so I could look nice. I even smiled, but deep down inside I was scared. And people could tell. I think that's why they tried to hurt me. Many people, including the alcoholic in my life, made things worse by constantly criticizing me. To survive I had to learn how to ignore criticism that came from sick people. And I had to learn how to give myself compliments.

It's been good for me to give myself three compliments every day. At first I didn't believe any of the good things that I said to myself. But eventually the messages got deep down into my soul, and they helped. I still feel awkward and insecure, but I'm learning how to love myself, even when it feels like no one else in my family loves me. Thanks, Alateens, for letting me know there's hope and for letting me know I'm not really alone.

I'm a runaway. It started when I was a small child. I began to hide in closets or outside in the yard. It steadily progressed from being missing for an hour to being missing for a day. Then it became days and even weeks. Finally it became months. Anytime I was afraid or scared of the alcoholics in my life, I left. I was terrified of their reactions. I could always feel the tension bubbling up in the house. That's what told me it was time to leave.

In Alateen I've learned that facing my problems is the best

solution, because no matter how far I run, the problem will always follow me. I've begun to use the slogan, Let Go and Let God. My Higher Power helps me face the mean monsters that I've been running from.

Today, I still feel tempted to run or procrastinate. Someday I'll stop completely. In the meantime, I'm using the slogans and the Twelve Steps to help me get better.

✍️

I think Alateen helps me most when I'm feeling afraid. Sometimes things happen at home that I don't know how to deal with. It's really hard for me to carry the program home with me, so when things happen I get out my Alateen book and try to calm myself down until I can get to a meeting.

When I get to the meeting and tell my problem, the other Alateens share their experiences. I listen and get a lot of ideas and encouragement. If I didn't have Alateen I would be at home with feelings stored up inside of me, and I would be feeling very afraid. Now I know I can take care of my problems without being so crazy with fear.

✍️

When my mother discovered the relationship I was having with my boyfriend, she turned to my stepfather for advice. It turned into a three-way conflict. My stepfather beat my mother. Then he locked both of us out of the house. When we finally got back into the house, I discovered that I was locked out of my room. It was terrible. I felt awful.

Everything seemed like it was my fault. My mother sent me away to live with my grandparents. I'd never felt so unwanted in my whole life. My mother insisted that what she had done was for my own safety, but it didn't feel that way. Finally, I ended up going back to an Alateen meeting.

When the leader asked if anyone had any problems to discuss, I took a deep breath and started to talk. Everybody was very supportive. They shared their ideas with me. I started really using my program after that meeting. Now when my stepfather starts going off the deep end, I try to remember it's just the alcohol that's talking. If there's absolutely no one around for me to talk to, I can always whisper. My Higher Power is always there to listen, even if I can't talk out loud.

The biggest problem in my life was the problem that brought me into the program — my father's addictions. My father drank a lot before he left our family, and he also abused other drugs. There were always broken promises and fights. It seemed so normal to me for all of these things to keep happening.

My father did a lot of things that he will regret. Things like almost killing my brother for not taking out the garbage, or something stupid like that. Finally, my father left late one night — on my birthday. That was the best and the worst day of my life.

It was very hard to make it through all of these things that happened in my life. Alateen became absolutely essential to my survival. My first couple of years in Alateen, I didn't really work my program. I just kept coming back. I liked hearing other people talk about the same things that were happening to me. I didn't feel so alone anymore. As time passed, I found myself talking and helping others by doing the same kinds of things that people had done for me.

Alateen became the kind of place where I didn't have to

worry about what I said. I could just talk and be myself. I learned how to release my anger in safe ways. I wasn't hitting brick walls with my fists anymore. I wasn't hurting myself or others. Instead, I channeled my anger into making music or writing.

Probably the biggest help that I got with my problems was when Alateen showed me how to respect myself. All my life, people had told me that I should respect others. But Alateen was telling me that I needed to respect myself before I could even start to respect anyone else.

I feel better now than I have ever felt in my whole life. Each time I go to a meeting or read some of the literature, I feel even better. I can look back at where I was when I entered this program, and I feel like a completely different person. I have changed. And I keep getting better.

I haven't really been in Alateen that long, so I guess I don't have very much to say. Except, I have made one step toward solving my problems. And that is it's okay for me to know what my problems are.

Living with alcoholic parents has not been a good experience for me. I have a lot of anger built up inside of me. I'm just grateful that there are people out there who are like me and who understand me.

Being certified as an adult in criminal court and sent to prison for ten months when I was fifteen years old is the hardest thing I've ever had to deal with in my life. I'm still trying to deal with it, even though I've been out of prison for almost a year.

The Alateen program has helped me learn how to be more honest and sincere. Until getting into the program I never knew how easy it could be to get and to give real love. Thanks, Alateens, for giving me another chance in my life. Only this time it feels like I've got a real, good chance.

🖎

The things that really help me are the people, the hugs, and the love. The really weird thing about Alateen is it's hard for me to believe so many people love me.

🖎

Sometimes my father would take out his frustrations and hostilities on me. Maybe he did that because he was angry at himself. He'd insult me and put me down for who I was. But I wasn't so bad, after all.

Thanks to Alateen, I know that I'm a valuable person. The problem is sometimes I forget what I've learned in the program. Sometimes I just need to talk about the way things used to be, so maybe I can remember that that was then, and now is now.

🖎

When my dad went into the hospital for the first time to get help with his drinking, I had a lot of expectations. In Alateen I learned to let go of my expectations, because not everything turns out the way I think it's supposed to. Alateen has helped me the most by giving me pages to read, slogans to think about, and just a lot of real good talking. In Alateen I've learned to take life one day at a time.

Even though she is sober, my mother still rejects me. Sobriety does not cure everything, since the physical part of the drinking is only one part of alcoholism. In fact she used to be verbally and emotionally abusive, and she still is. Also, my parents divorced, and my father distanced himself from me too.

My family life hasn't improved even since my mother got sober. I'm learning in Alateen that if I want to be happy, I have to forget about my parents getting back together. I have to forget about my dreams of having the perfect parents. I just have to keep taking good care of myself, as good as I can.

My father sent me away on vacation, and when I came back he and my stepmother were already married. I couldn't believe he would do that. It wouldn't have hurt so much if I'd been 100% sure that he knew what he was doing. He wasn't in Alcoholics Anonymous yet, and I hadn't started Alateen so I didn't know how to tell him about my feelings.

A couple of years later, I joined Alateen. I still resented my dad for what he had done to me. I talked about it with my group. I couldn't believe how much difference that made. My pain went away. I don't know how it works, but it works.

One experience that hurt me was when my parents got a divorce. Another was when I was five years old and I saw my father beat my mom. I also went through a lot of custody battles. I didn't have a lot of fun when I was younger, but I have a lot of fun in Alateen now. I live one day at a time, and I still care about a lot of people.

Both of my parents are alcoholics. When I was younger they would always go out with their friends and leave me home alone. It was very scary. I used to wait up for them to make sure they got home okay, but now I just go to bed. I know when they come home anyway, because they always wake me up with all of their noise.

Now I have a friend over once in a while. The other day when we were there my mom called to tell us to go to my room and lock the door. She said my dad was going to come home very drunk and very mad, and when she was talking to me on the phone he came in the door. My friend and I went into my room. We could hear my dad throwing things and breaking things all over the house. We got out of there fast. I stayed at my friend's house that night. I don't know how much worse it has to get before my dad and my mom will finally get some help.

My father left my brother, sister, mother and me. He left because he and my mom fought so much about his alcoholism. I'm mad at my father. I really can't mean it when I say, "I love you, Dad," because I don't know him.

He left us when my sister and I were two and my brother was one. I regret not having a father around when I was little. I still regret not having him around today. I always wonder what it would be like if my father was there then and now. But I'm also glad that he wasn't and isn't there, because I like the way my mom raised me.

We aren't a so-called normal family. We have an open relationship. I talk with my mom about almost everything. She understands me because she hasn't forgotten what it's like to be a kid. I want to thank my mom for everything she's done for me. And I would like to get to know my father, because someday I would like to say, "I love you, Dad," and mean it.

I used to deal with all of my problems by running away or by destroying things. Alateen showed me how to deal with my problems, calmly. I learned how to buy myself some time to think about what I was going to do before I started taking action.

I don't run away anymore. The only thing I've destroyed is my pillow. I use it for a punching bag. My frustrations are a lot safer to handle when I use a pillow instead of somebody's head.

I've made a lot of friends in Alateen. They're easy to relate to. I can talk to them about my problems without feeling like a fool. The difference in me is noticeable to everyone who knew me before I came to Alateen.

The difference is also very noticeable to me. I'm a much happier person today. I'm glad I found Alateen.

Workshop On
WORKING TOWARD SOLUTIONS

Complete the following sentences, adding as many sentences as you want.

Alateen helped me to work through a problem by ...

The parts of the program that helped me the most in finding solutions are ...

The sharing I most relate to is ...

I relate to it because ...

WHAT MAKES YOU FEEL HAPPY?
WHAT MAKES YOU FEEL SAD?

When we reflect back on our week it is easy to concentrate on the bad events, our difficulties, and our problems. The good things escape us. When we start to think about what makes us sad, about our disappointments, it's important to balance them with the good things that happen. Often we can't think of anything good at all. Some people force themselves to talk about one good thing for each and every sad thing. Gradually we learn that our lives in the program are filled with "happys." We just have to look for them.

Alateens share on
WHAT MAKES YOU FEEL HAPPY?
WHAT MAKES YOU FEEL SAD?

Encouragement makes me feel happy. Arguments make me feel sad.

✍🏻

In our Alateen group we use an Alateen Rap after we've read the Steps and after we've said the Serenity Prayer. It helps us relax enough to be able to share what's been happening with us. So, here it goes: "Was it glad? Was it rad? Was it happy? Was it sad? Come on, kids; tell us what kind of week you had. Was it glad? Was it rad? Was it happy? Was it sad?"

✍

I feel happy when I have succeeded at something, like when I get good grades. I also feel happy when I go to an Alateen meeting, because of the welcome and love and respect I get from the other members. I feel sad when I get rejected or when I have failed at something.

✍

Camping makes me feel happy. One sad thing is knowing I've hurt a lot of people.

✍

One thing that makes me feel happy is when I get a phone call from someone I haven't heard from in a long time. Something that makes me feel sad is when I get cut down and I can't say anything about it.

✍

DRINKING AND DAD

Dad, you made the decision to take the first drink,
Now you're so hooked it messes up the way you
think.
Every time I see you, you've got a buzz,
I never understood why, no one really does.
For a long time I had no idea what to do,
The program helps me understand no one can stop
you but you.

I wish there was something I could do to help,
I can only pray for you, Dad, and try to help
myself.
I use the prayer to help me through my day,
Thanks to the Steps, program, and the prayer,
They made me the healthy person I am today.

I feel happy when I see babies. I feel happy when I see people being nice to each other. I feel sad when I'm looking at things I've recently lost. Also, I feel sad when I witness discrimination against other people.

☞

When my father isn't drinking I feel happy. When I'm at an Alateen meeting I feel happy, because I can tell how I'm feeling and I know I won't be laughed at. On the other hand, when my father is drinking I feel very sad. And when I can't tell anyone how I'm feeling it makes me mad.

✍

Some of the things that make me happy are: talking to my friends, drawing and reading a book. Some of the things that make me sad are when my parents and I and my brother and my friends get into fights.

✍

I feel happy when I make people laugh. That way, I feel at least one more person is happy today. I feel sad when I fight with my family. It leaves an internal scar that gets cut open every time I fight with them.

✍

Something that makes me happy is when I'm away from my mom when she is drunk. Things that make me feel sad are when I get into trouble and when my mom is drunk.

✍

Being able to listen to people and help them makes me feel happy. Listening to my mother and seeing her totally wasted really hurts me. I feel sad because she doesn't realize what she's doing to herself and to me and to everybody else.

Some of the things that make me happy are: friends; Alateen; playing baseball; going to school. Something that makes me sad is when something happens at home and no one can take me to my Alateen meeting.

Things that make me feel happy are: watching my mom and dad talk and reason things out; watching my brother have a good time without drugs or alcohol. Some of the things that make me feel sad are: watching my dad drink; watching people be stupid on TV.

Some of the things that make me happy are: sports; camping; getting my feelings out. Things that make me sad are: getting into trouble; and when people make fun of me.

I'm happy and sad at the same time, about holidays. I'm happy because I like being surprised with presents. I'm sad because we're poorer than we were last year. I'm also happy because I have a family to share the holidays with.

It makes me happy to know that I've done my best. It makes me sad when I can't control what's going on.

I feel happy when I'm helping others in their hardships and trying times. When I feel like the chaotic world that I used to live in is coming back, then I feel sad.

✍

I'm sad because my friend is really, really sad. This is her first birthday without her mom alive to celebrate with her and her brother and her dad. I can't even think of my mom dying. I don't want to know how hard that would be.

✍

I feel happy when I'm playing an important part in other people's lives. I feel sad when I feel responsible for making others upset or angry.

✍

I feel happy when I feel loved. I feel sad when I know I can't succeed at something I want to do.

✍

When I pick a wildflower and put it behind my ear, I feel happy. When I feel like giving up on something, I feel sad.

✍

I feel sad when somebody tells me what to do. I feel happy when I have choices.

I feel happy because my parents aren't drinking anymore. I also feel happy because I get to go to a lot of Alateen meetings. At meetings I get to share my feelings with everybody without getting my feelings hurt. I feel sad because I hardly ever get to see my dad.

I feel happy when my family and I are doing something together. I feel sad when my father drinks.

One of the things that make me happy is a big ol' thunderstorm. I feel more relaxed during a thunderstorm. For some reason, I feel jumpy and hyper when the sun is shining.

What makes me happy is that my parents had enough courage to face their disease and not deny it, so they didn't make things worse. What makes me sad is my parents will never be cured. Also, my sister and I have a better chance of becoming alcoholics if we ever start to drink.

I feel happy when I do something nice for someone. I feel sad when people put me down, or when they talk about me.

Workshop On
WHAT MAKES YOU FEEL HAPPY?
WHAT MAKES YOU FEEL SAD?

Complete the following sentences adding as many as many sentences as you want.

The things that make me happy are ...

The things that make me sad are ...

If I feel sad, I can ...

When I don't know how to feel, I can ...

HOW WAS YOUR WEEK?

Sometimes it's difficult to relate to and discuss abstract program topics. Usually the real events of our lives are easier to talk about. Meetings often use the following format: "On a scale of one to ten (one being the worst, and ten being perfect), how would you score your week? Also, would you share one good thing that happened this week, and one bad thing that happened this week?" This helps start discussion and maintain balance between positive and negative sharings.

Alateens share on
HOW WAS YOUR WEEK

I would consider this week in my life a six. Even though I did some bad things, a lot of growing has come out of it. I think in this week, alone, I've probably used all of the Twelve Steps in one way or another.

The good thing is that my parents seem to have a better understanding of me. But the bad thing is that they don't trust me. They know when I make a mistake, but they don't seem to realize that I'm learning from my mistakes. They think I'm just going to keep on making the same mistakes all the time.

I'd give this week a nine. I got a very good report card. The bad thing that happened this week is that my alcoholic father is trying to mess up my life. The good thing is, I'm learning how to handle my anger.

✍️

On a scale of one to ten, I think this week was a six. We went on vacation and had a good time in the sunshine. That was the good thing that happened. The bad thing is that we stayed with my grandfather. My grandfather is a drunk. The worst part is that he acts like a drunk even when he isn't drinking. Another good thing, though — he gave our family another chance to work our own programs. It really does work, when you work it.

✍️

Before I came to Alateen I didn't understand why my parents drank. Now I understand better, and I feel better. This week I would score about an eight. The best thing that happened this week is my team won a ball game, 22-17. The bad thing that happened is we lost a ball game to my teachers.

✍

I give this week a six. One good thing that happened is I communicated with both my mom and my dad in a loving way. One bad thing is I watched a thirty-year-old give alcohol to a three-year-old. I didn't try to stop it from happening, whether I could have or not.

Before I came to Alateen I wasn't able to work out my problems by myself. I just couldn't stand up for myself. Now that I've been in the program for over two years, I've learned to deal with some of my problems and to fight back when I need to. So now I don't feel as depressed as I used to feel.

✍

On a scale from one (worst) to ten (best), I would score my week about two or three. The reason is — How would you rate your week if you got into a bike wreck?

✍

I'm having a very good week. I'd score it about a seven. Today I feel good about myself because I've done my part to live one day at a time. I don't think about the future very much. If I feel depressed or unhappy I can always turn to my Higher Power. I keep coming back to Alateen because I have more questions to be answered. Sometimes I feel scared about coming back, but I've started sharing more and helping the newcomers. That seems to help me.

✍

I'd give my week almost a ten. The good thing that's happened is that I've met all these new people at an Alateen conference. The bad thing is I didn't get any sleep.

✍

If I had to rate my week, it would have to be a six. It's been a bad week. My mom got laid off from her job, and I'm still going to court over something that happened four years ago. The only good thing about this week is that I was at my first Alateen conference, and I loved it.

✍

My week has been about a three. A bad thing that happened is I found out I have a major depression. Now I have to go on medicine, and I have to go to all of these different doctors. I hate doing all that.

My parents are both alcoholics, and they don't get along with each other. Their relationship is very stressful for me. Of course, the doctors say I should avoid stress. I know I have to detach, but I'm new to Alateen — so that's very difficult for me to do right now. One good thing is my coming to Alateen. It's helping me to get my feelings out in the open. It's the only place I've ever found where I can do that. So that's why I keep coming back to Alateen.

I would score my week about a three. I feel like my friends are too involved in my life right now. My father is blaming me for the death of our family dog.

The bad thing that happened this week was that I got upset after seeing a dog that reminded me of mine. The good thing that happened is that I got to go to an Alateen convention.

This week was a very good one for me. I'd give it about an eight. The good thing that happened is that I got invited three times to go swimming at my neighbor's swimming pool. I helped my neighbor's granddaughter learn how to dive. The bad thing that happened is I got in a fight with my mom, and I lied to her.

Workshop On
HOW WAS YOUR WEEK

Complete the following sentences, adding as many sentences as you want.

On a scale of one to ten (1 being pretty bad, and 10 being almost perfect) I'd rate my week about ...

The reason why I would give my week this score is ...

One of the good things that happened during my week is...

One of the bad things that happened during my week is ...

The Alateen program helps me with my week because ...

REFLECTIONS

REMEMBER!

1. We have been brought together by one common problem; let us concentrate on that. Alcoholism has impacted all of our lives. Let's concentrate on sharing our experience, strength and hope so we can find contentment and even happiness, whether the alcoholics are still drinking or not.

2. Let's resist the temptation to gossip, and let's discourage it in others. Especially, let's avoid hurting anyone in our group, because anything that hurts one member hurts our whole group.

3. Let's remember to ask each other about what we're doing before we do it. Although members may be given certain responsibilities, all are equal. Each of us has a vote.

4. Let's be patient with those who are slow to grasp the principles of the Alateen program. Each person progresses in his or her own way. We help each other by sharing our experience, strength and hope.

5. Always remember that Alateen meetings are working sessions. Let's make the best use of the time we have.

6. Keep in confidence everything that is said at meetings. If members are assured that what they tell will not be revealed outside the group, they will feel encouraged to speak freely. Knowing that "you can tell anything" to fellow Alateens will have rich rewards for all. Remember, the friends you make in Alateen are special.

from *Alateen — Hope for Children of Alcoholics,* page 102, revised and adapted 1996)

A FINAL WORD

I think I was destined to be in an alcoholic home. I am so grateful for that because I could not have received the blessings from this program if it wasn't for my mother, the alcoholic in my family. I remember the times when I would come home from school and she wouldn't be there. I'd sit out on the front lawn waiting for her but she wouldn't show. She chose the booze and drugs over me, over her own child. That hurt me a lot. She just didn't understand what she was doing. Although my mother was very unfit, I still loved her with all my heart and soul.

Finally the disease got her and she passed away. That was very hard for me. I mourned over my mother's death and was very suicidal. I blamed God for taking my mother away and started rebelling against Him. At twelve I got into the Alateen program but had not yet forgiven my Higher Power. I didn't want to because I was still very angry and suicidal.

I needed the unconditional love I got in Alateen because I didn't have it all through my childhood. That love gave me a sense of security — it was my security blanket.

In my first year of the program I went to an Alateen conference. It was a weekend where you could just go away and "Let Go and Let God." That came to be my first slogan that I really liked a lot because it kind of related to my mom's death. The idea that I could let go of her and let God handle everything helped me. I felt I could turn to my Higher Power and between the first and second year in program I finally accepted him back in my life. I had to find something higher than myself. Someone I could turn to when things were going wrong or when it seemed that things were falling apart. My brothers were using drugs and alcohol. As I got further into the program, I learned to accept that I couldn't do anything about it. I learned that the only person I could change was me.

I'm in my sixth year of the program and oh so grateful for it. It has given me so much and helped me move on. It's been like my guiding light, my path. I don't have to sit on my pity pot saying "Oh, my mother's gone and my brothers are alcoholics." I know it's okay, I just need to focus on myself. Just for today I can go on living a "normal" childhood. There are a lot of things in my life that I wish I could have changed or made better but I can't. It's not easy growing up in an alcoholic home and having your mother pass away so soon. But, it's something I've learned to deal with. It's okay sometimes to sit down and cry and it's okay sometimes to just get mad at whatever. I always have something to look forward to now. There are things yet to come, and I have learned to appreciate the things I do have in my life.

Even though you have an alcoholic in your family, there's still a way, it's not over. That's why I'm so grateful for this program because I thought it was over at one point in my life. I thought everything was just going to fall down on me and I was going to hit rock bottom and it was going to be over. But it's not over and it won't be over. This is my security blanket and it's always going to be here for me. No matter what happens to me, whatever I do, wherever I go, this program is going to be with me, forever.

Alateen has given me a new beginning and a new life. I know there is hope for children of alcoholics. I know that I am not alone and there are other kids out there that have alcoholic parents and are living with this disease.

I know now that I can go on and that my life isn't going to end tomorrow just because my parents are alcoholics. Thank you Alateen for giving me the world. I couldn't ever ask for more.

Al-Anon/Alateen Declaration

**When anyone, anywhere, reaches out for help
let the hand of Al-Anon and Alateen
always be there, and — *Let It Begin With Me.***

AL-ANON'S TWELVE CONCEPTS OF SERVICE

The Twelve Steps and Traditions are guides for personal growth and group unity. The Twelve Concepts are guides for service. They show how Al-Anon and Alateen Twelfth Step work can be done on a broad scale and how members of a World Service Office can relate to each other and to the groups, through a World Service Conference, to spread the Al-Anon/Alateen message worldwide.

1. The ultimate responsibility and authority for Al-Anon world services belongs to the Al-Anon groups.
2. The Al-Anon Family Groups have delegated complete administrative and operational authority to their Conference and its service arms.
3. The right of Decision makes effective leadership possible.
4. Participation is the key to harmony.
5. The Rights of Appeal and Petition protect minorities and assure that they be heard.
6. The Conference acknowledges the primary administrative responsibility of the trustees.
7. The trustees have legal rights while the rights of the Conference are traditional.
8. The Board of Trustees delegates full authority for routine management of the Al-Anon Headquarters to its executive committees.
9. Good personal leadership at all service levels is a necessity. In the field of world service the Board of Trustees assumes the primary leadership.
10. Service responsibility is balanced by carefully defined service authority and double-headed management is avoided.

11. The World Service Office is composed of standing committees, executives and staff members.
12. The spiritual foundation for Al-Anon's world service is contained in the General Warranties of the Conference, Article 12 of the Charter.

GENERAL WARRANTIES

In all its proceedings the World Service Conference of Al-Anon shall observe the spirit of the Traditions:

1. that only sufficient operating funds, including an ample reserve, be its prudent financial principle;
2. that no Conference member shall be placed in unqualified authority over other members;
3. that all decisions be reached by discussion, vote and, whenever possible, by unanimity;
4. that no Conference action ever be personally punitive or an incitement to public controversy;
5. that though the Conference serves Al-Anon, it shall never perform any act of government; and that, like the fellowship of Al-Anon Family Groups which it serves, it shall always remain democratic in thought and action.

INDEX

A

Abandonment 44
Abuse 34, 39, 49, 54, 71, 94, 95, 103, 118, 126, 167, 205, 290, 292, 296
Acceptance 41, 78, 91, 92, 94, 96, 98, 103, 104, 105, 108, 119, 123, 127, 130, 134, 135, 151, 170, 172, 175, 282, 283, 284, 285, 287, 287, 316
Active alcoholism 92, 99, 103-105, 136
Advice 248, 267
Al-Anon 66, 85, 96, 110, 133, 139, 163, 174, 201, 204, 210, 212, 213, 218, 220, 225, 226, 227, 228, 230, 235, 238, 239, 240, 241, 250, 251, 252, 258, 262, 265, 270, 271, 287, 289, 313, 317
Al-Anon/Alateen Declaration 208
Alateen—A Day at a Time 24
Alateen—Hope for Children of Alcoholics 24, 47, 267, 314
Alateen in general 4, 9, 11, 173, 183, 189, 196, 204
Alateen in schools 179, 202
Alcoholics Anonymous 10, 11, 27, 28, 35, 44, 50-51, 96, 110, 155, 163, 177, 180, 213, 216, 218, 220, 225, 226, 227, 228, 230, 235, 248, 254, 257, 264, 270, 296
Alcoholism 10, 11, 14, 32, 36, 37, 41, 43, 48, 49, 50, 57, 71, 73, 91, 92, 95, 96 107, 115, 123, 131, 136, 144, 156, 167, 171, 178, 179, 194, 205, 207, 217, 220, 223, 239, 248, 250, 251, 256, 260, 265, 271, 274, 275, 278, 283, 285, 288, 289, 290, 296, 297, 306, 310, 314, 315, 317
Amends 86, 89, 148-152, 153-158
Anger 26, 43, 46, 54, 56, 67, 71, 75, 104, 118, 129, 131, 139, 140, 145, 146, 148, 156, 167, 192, 223, 275, 281, 282, 285, 287, 289, 294, 295, 297, 305, 309, 316
Anonymity 186, 211, 225, 238, 250, 251, 252, 254-259, 260-68
Asking for help 42, 218, 270, 272, 289
Assemblies 154, 210, 235, 241, 246, 256, 261
Attitudes 119, 163, 235
Autonomy 17, 210-215

B

Beauty 130
Beginners see Newcomers
Belonging 223, 251, 282, 291
Blame 30, 34, 36, 37, 42, 91, 95, 115, 127, 223, 289, 312

C

Carrying the message 89, 90, 174, 238, 254, 256, 264, 272, 263, 287, 294, 316
Change 41, 95, 99, 131, 134, 135, 146, 148, 159, 168, 169, 173, 213, 263, 270, 282, 287, 288, 294, 316
Changed attitudes 95, 131, 163, 277
Choices 96, 97, 114, 285, 297, 305
Cliques 249, 264
Closing, Alateen 21-2
Communication 59, 207, 271, 310
Conferences/Conventions 154, 157, 192, 202, 235, 236, 311, 315
Confidence 124, 314
Confidentiality

G

H

I

J

K